Lab Manual for i-Net+ Guide to the Internet

Clint Saxton

COURSE
TECHNOLOGY
TM
THOMSON LEARNING

Australia • Canada • Mexico • Singapore • Spain • United Kingdom • United States

COURSE TECHNOLOGY
™
THOMSON LEARNING

Lab Manual for i-Net+ Guide to the Internet
is published by Course Technology.

Associate Publisher:
Steve Elliot

Product Manager:
Amy M. Lyon

Developmental Editor:
Jill Batistick

Production Editor:
Daphne E. Barbas

Manufacturing Coordinator:
Alexander Schall

Quality Assurance Technical Lead:
Nicole Ashton

Associate Product Manager:
Tim Gleeson

Editorial Assistant:
Nick Lombardi

Marketing Manager:
Toby Shelton

Text Designer:
GEX Publishing Services

Compositor:
GEX Publishing Services

Cover Design:
Abby Schol

BRIEF
Contents

TABLE OF

Contents

Introduction

This lab manual assumes no previous knowledge of i-Net+ material and was designed to prepare you for the CompTIA i-Net+ certification exam. The manual is designed for use in conjunction with the *i-Net+ Guide to the Internet, Second Edition* (0-619-12068-1), but it also can be used to supplement any i-Net+ courseware. This manual is best utilized in a classroom lab environment but it may also be helpful for self-study on a home network.

Uniquely designed with you in mind, this lab manual is written from the "show-me" perspective—instead of simply describing a procedure or task, this manual shows you how to complete it, step by step. Whether writing a script, or writing a Web page, each lab encourages hands-on interaction and logically guides you through learning the i-Net+ certification objectives. In conjunction with *i-Net+ Guide to the Internet, Second Edition* (0-619-12068-1), there is no better way to prepare for the CompTIA i-Net+ certification exam.

FEATURES

In order to ensure a successful experience for instructors and students alike, this book includes the following features:

- **i-Net+ Certification Objectives**—For each chapter, the relevant objectives from the CompTIA iNet+ exam are listed.
- **Lab Objectives**—Every lab has a brief description and list of learning objectives.
- **Materials Required**—Every lab includes information on hardware, software, and other materials you will need to complete the lab.
- **Completion Times**—Every lab has an estimated completion time, so that you can plan your activities more accurately.
- **Activity Sections**—Labs are presented in manageable sections. Where appropriate, additional Activity Background information is provided to illustrate the importance of a particular project.
- **Step-by-Step Instructions**—This section provides steps to enhance technical proficiency.
- **Review Questions**—Questions help reinforce concepts presented in the lab.

Note for Instructors: Answers to review questions are available on the Course Technology web site at www.course.com/irk/. Search on this book's ISBN, which is found on the back cover.

HARDWARE REQUIREMENTS

- A Pentium 166 MHz CPU or higher (300 MHz recommended)
- 32 MB of RAM minimum (64 MB recommended)
- A 2 GB hard disk with at least 500 MB of available storage space (4 GB hard disk or larger with at least 1 GB available storage space recommended)
- A CD-ROM drive
- A modem or some other available connection to the Internet (Cable, DSL, or faster preferred)
- A printer (optional)
- A network interface card

SOFTWARE/SETUP REQUIREMENTS

- Windows 98
- Internet Browser (Internet Explorer 5.0 or later)
- An intranet or Internet Web Share (in a classroom environment, this can be a desktop computer running web server software and providing student shares)

ABOUT THE AUTHOR

Clint Saxton has earned a solid reputation in the Information Technology field through his mastery of computer hardware, software, programming, and networking. His career has encompassed many aspects of IT, including desktop server support, infrastructure administration, software development, training, and networking. He brings this breadth and depth of knowledge to the *Lab Manual for i-Net+ Guide to the Internet*.

ACKNOWLEDGMENTS

I would like to give special thanks to Amanda Hart, for her patience, support, and encouragement throughout this entire project. I also offer a heartfelt thanks to Peggy Linthicum, Roy Saxton, and my entire family, who have always been supportive and encouraging.

I extend my sincere appreciation to Jill Batistick, the Developmental Editor, who has done an excellent job and given a tireless effort to a very long project. At Course Technology I especially appreciate the efforts of Lisa Egan, Senior Editor, and Amy Lyon, Product Manager, who have both played instrumental roles in the publication of this lab manual. Many thanks also to the reviewers for their insights and valuable input. A sincere thank you to Ric Calhoun and Janos Fustos.

CHAPTER ONE

USING THE INTERNET

Labs included in this chapter

➤ Lab 1.1 Understanding Microsoft Internet Explorer

➤ Lab 1.2 Browsing the Web Using Internet Explorer

➤ Lab 1.3 Search Engines and Copyrights

➤ Lab 1.4 Researching Local Internet Service Providers (ISPs)

i-Net+ Exam Objectives	
Objective	Lab
Understand and be able to describe the infrastructure needed to support an Internet client.	1.1, 1.2, 1.4
Use/configure web browsers and other Internet/intranet clients, and be able to describe their use to others.	1.1, 1.2
Use different types of search indexes—static index/site map, keyword index, full text index.	1.3
Identify key factors relating to legal and regulatory considerations when planning e-business solutions.	1.3
Identify the issues that affect Internet site functionality.	1.4
Create a logic diagram of Internet components from the client to the server.	1.4
Describe various hardware and software connection devices and when to use them.	1.4

LAB 1.1 UNDERSTANDING MICROSOFT INTERNET EXPLORER

Objectives

The goal of this lab is to introduce you to Microsoft Internet Explorer and to develop a general understanding of client/server architecture.

To understand the environment in which this lab will operate, you need to know the following facts:

➤ A home page is the first web page that a web browser will attempt to display after it has been started. It is also the web page that will be displayed if you click the Home button found on the toolbar near the top of your browser window.

➤ A client is a software program or a computer that requests information (data) from another software program or computer.

➤ A web browser is a client software program that requests information from another program (the web server) on the WWW. Internet Explorer is an example of a web browser.

➤ A server can be either a software program or a computer that has been designed to "serve up" or respond to a client request. For example, when you access a web page on the World Wide Web (WWW), both your computer and your web browser are making client requests to a web server. If the server is functioning properly, both the web server software program and the server computer will respond by sending your computer, and your web browser, the information (data) necessary to display the requested web page.

After completing this lab, you will be able to:

➤ Configure Microsoft Internet Explorer to use a home page

➤ Describe the difference between a client and a server

Materials Required

➤ Windows 9x or Windows 2000 Professional

➤ A lab workgroup size of 2–4 students

➤ Microsoft Internet Explorer 5 or later installed on each lab computer

➤ A shortcut to Internet Explorer on the desktop of each lab computer

➤ A configured home page (that is, not blank) for each lab computer

Estimated completion time: **30 minutes**

ACTIVITY

Starting Internet Explorer:

1. To start Internet Explorer, double-click the **Internet Explorer** icon on your desktop. Figure 1-1 shows Internet Explorer open to the MCI WordCom web site. Your browser may be configured to view a different web site.

Close button

Figure 1-1   A sample page opened in Internet Explorer

2. Click the **Close** button.

Configuring a different home page:

1. Double-click the **Internet Explorer** icon found on your desktop.

2. In the browser window, click **Tools** on the menu bar, and then click **Internet Options**.

3. On the line provided below, write the web address found in the Address box. The address you write down is the home page that Internet Explorer is currently configured to use.

4. Click the **Use Blank** button. Notice that the text in the Address box has now changed to "about:blank."

5. Click the **OK** button. The change you have made to the home page address will be saved.

6. Click the **Close** button of the browser window.

Testing the configuration change:

1. Double-click the **Internet Explorer** icon on your desktop. Notice that your web browser now displays a blank web page.

2. Click the **Close** button of the browser window to close Internet Explorer.

Certification Objectives:

Objectives for the i-Net+ exam:

➤ Understand and be able to describe the infrastructure needed to support an Internet client.

➤ Use/configure web browsers and other Internet/intranet clients, and be able to describe their use to others.

Review Questions

1. Internet Explorer is an example of a web browser. True or False?

2. A home page cannot be configured by the user. True or False?

3. A web browser, like Internet Explorer, is an example of a client software program. True or False?

4. The WWW is an accumulation of information stored on two large computers called the Internet Web Servers. True or False?

5. At work, when Amanda starts Internet Explorer, the company's web page is displayed. Amanda would like to configure her home computer to open to the same web page. On the lines provided, describe the changes Amanda must make to reconfigure her web browser so that *http://www.yahoo.com* will be displayed when she starts Internet Explorer.

_____

_____

_____

_____

_____

LAB 1.2 BROWSING THE WEB USING INTERNET EXPLORER

Objectives

The goal of this lab is to build on your knowledge of Internet Explorer and begin browsing the WWW. We begin by examining the parts of the URL. Then, we explore the buttons and other options that you will use with Internet Explorer. Through these activities, you will gain insight into what your computer is doing when you "surf the Web."

The Hypertext Markup Language (HTML) is a markup language used for hypertext documents on the WWW. The language uses tags to format the document, create hyperlinks, and mark locations for graphics. In later activities, you will be using HTML to create web pages.

Hypertext is text in a document, or web page, that has been written in HTML format. Most web pages are some form of a hypertext document and can contain hyperlinks, that, when clicked, redirect a web browser to different URLs.

A hyperlink is a tag in a hypertext document that links the location of the tag to another point in the same document or to an entirely different document. For example, if Course Technology wanted to create a link to the Microsoft web site, they would simply create a hyperlink containing the URL for the Microsoft web site. When a user clicked that hyperlink, the web browser would be redirected to the Microsoft web site. Hyperlinks are sometimes referred to as hot links or links.

A protocol is a set of rules for communication used by a computer program. Some common forms of communication, or protocols, used on the Internet include the Hypertext Transfer Protocol (HTTP), the File Transfer Protocol (FTP), Telnet, and the Internet Relay Chat (IRC). These protocols will be explored further in later chapters of this lab manual.

When you type a URL into your browser or click a Favorite, the web browser sends a GET request to the web server. The web server interprets the request and returns all of the data for the requested web page.

A uniform resource locator (URL) is an address for a resource on the Internet. A URL can contain the protocol used by the resource, the name of the computer, and the path and name of a file on the computer. Most often, the computer that is named in the URL is a server. Examine Figure 1–2 for more information.

Figure 1-2   A URL contains the protocol used, the host name of the web server and the path and filename of the requested file

After completing this lab, you will be able to:

➤ Describe how a URL is formed and identify malformed URLs

➤ Describe and use various Internet Explorer toolbar buttons

➤ Use and create a Favorite

Materials Required

This lab will require the following:

➤ Windows 9x or Windows 2000 Professional

➤ A lab workgroup size of 2–4 students

➤ Microsoft Internet Explorer 5.0 or later

➤ Access to the Internet for each computer

➤ A shortcut to Internet Explorer on the desktop

Estimated completion time: **45 minutes**

ACTIVITY

Understanding URLs:

1. List the protocol name, host name (computer name), folder name(s), and filename for the following URLs:

   http://www.course.com/pcrepair/testing_urls.htm

   Protocol:

   _____

   Host name:

   _____

   Folder name(s):

   _____

   _____

   Filename:

   _____

http://www.yahoo.com/myfiles/uun/ac/main.html
Protocol:

_____

Host name:

_____

Folder name(s):

_____

_____

Filename:

_____

http://www.microsoft.com/anon/test/test2/test_users
Protocol:

_____

Host name:

_____

Folder name(s):

_____

_____

Filename:

_____

ftp://microsoft.com/anon/main.html
Protocol:

_____

Host name:

_____

Folder name(s):

_____

_____

Filename:

_____

Using the Forward and Back buttons:

1. Double-click the **Internet Explorer** icon on your desktop.

2. Click the **Address** box, type **http://www.microsoft.com**, and then press **Enter**. The Address box, the Forward button, and the Back button can be seen in Figure 1-3.

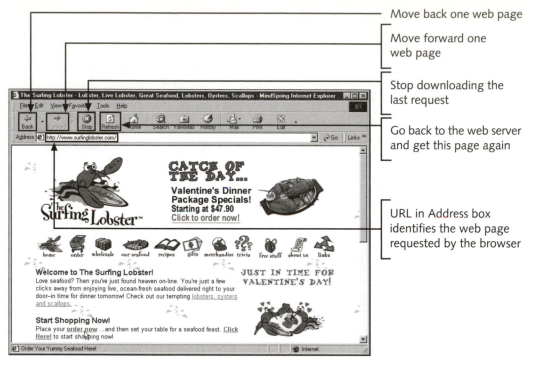

Figure 1-3   Navigating tools using Internet Explorer 5

3. Click the **Back** button on the Internet Explorer toolbar. On the line provided, describe how your browser responded.

_____

4. Click the **Forward** button on the Internet Explorer toolbar. On the line provided, describe how your browser responded.

_____

5. Close Internet Explorer.

Using the Stop and Refresh buttons:

1. Double-click the **Internet Explorer** icon on your desktop.

2. Click the **Address** box, type **http://www.microsoft.com**, and then press **Enter**.

3. Click the **Refresh** button on the Internet Explorer toolbar. (The button has the word "Refresh" on it.) On the line provided, describe how your browser responded.

_____

1

4. Click the **Refresh** button again, and immediately click the **Stop** button (it has the word "Stop" on it). On the line provided, describe how your browser responded.

_____

5. Close Internet Explorer.

Creating a Favorite:

1. Double-click the **Internet Explorer** icon on your desktop.

2. Click the **Address** box, type **http://www.course.com**, and then press **Enter**.

3. Click **Favorites** on the menu bar, and then click **Add to Favorites**. The Add Favorite dialog box opens. Your screen should look similar to Figure 1-4.

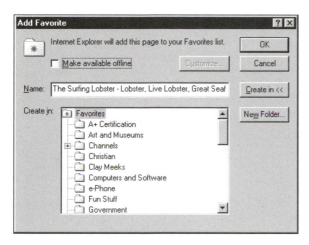

Figure 1-4   Add a favorite web site to the list of favorites

4. Click the **New Folder** button.

5. Click the **Folder name** text box, type **Publishers**, and then click the **OK** button.

6. Click the **Publishers** folder to highlight it, and then click the **OK** button. You have just created a Favorite to the Course Technology web site in a folder named Publishers.

7. Close Internet Explorer.

Using the Favorite you created:

1. Double-click the **Internet Explorer** icon on your desktop.

2. Click **Favorites** on the menu bar.

3. Click the **Publishers** folder, and then click the **Course Technology** favorite. The Course Technology web site should begin to load. As you can see, a Favorite is a shortcut to a web site. With Favorites, you can easily access your favorite web sites without having to remember the URLs.

4. Close Internet Explorer.

Using your History list:

1. Double-click the **Internet Explorer** icon on your desktop.

2. Click the **Address box** list arrow. A list of recently accessed URLs displays. This list is known as your History.

3. Click **http://www.microsoft.com**. The Microsoft web site will begin to load. As you can see, the History is a great way to quickly access recently used URLs.

4. Close Internet Explorer.

Certification Objectives:

Objectives for the i-Net+ exam:

➤ Understand and be able to describe the infrastructure needed to support an Internet client.

➤ Use/configure web browsers and other Internet/intranet clients, and be able to describe their use to others.

Review Questions

1. FTP and HTTP are both _____ used on the Internet.

2. A hyperlink is a way of "linking" to a different URL on the Internet. True or False?

3. Only two protocols are used on the Internet. True or False?

4. The only file in *http://www.altavista.com/001/002/htmltest.htm* is testhtml.htm. True or False?

5. A Favorite is shortcut to web document. True or False?

6. On the line provided, describe the relationship between HTML and HTTP.

_____

_____

_____

_____

_____

1

LAB 1.3 SEARCH ENGINES AND COPYRIGHTS

Objectives

The goal of this lab is to provide hands-on experience using search engines. You will also learn about copyright laws and how to protect intellectual property.

A copyright is the legal term used to describe protection offered to the creators of intellectual property; that protection gives the creator, and no one else, the right to copy, distribute, display, or perform the work. It is important to note that copyright laws do not protect an invention. On the other hand, a trademark is a name, symbol, or other mark that is used to represent a product or company.

There are many different ways to control and restrict a search; however, operators and methods vary depending on the search engine. To find out more information about your favorite search engine, check the help menu on their web site. Most search engines do allow the use of the "+" operator to include content in a search and the use of the "-" operator to exclude content from a search.

After completing this lab, you will be able to:

➤ Complete advanced searches using various Internet search engines

➤ Discuss how copyright laws affect intellectual property

➤ Add the copyright symbol to a web page

➤ Add the trademark symbol to a web page

Materials Required

This lab will require the following:

➤ Windows 9x

➤ A lab workgroup size of 2–4 students

➤ Microsoft Internet Explorer 5 or later

➤ A connection to the Internet

➤ Minimal HTML experience

Estimated completion time: **30 minutes**

ACTIVITY

Requiring content in search engine results:

1. Double-click the **Internet Explorer** icon on your desktop.

2. Type **http://www.yahoo.com** in the Address bar, and then press **Enter**.

3. In the Search for text box, type **+"president"+"Bush"**, and then press **Enter**.

4. Close Internet Explorer.

Excluding content from search engine results:

1. Double-click the **Internet Explorer** icon found on your desktop.

2. Type **http://www.yahoo.com** in the Address bar, and then press Enter.

3. In the Search for text box, type **+"president"–"Bush"**, and then press **Enter**.

4. Close Internet Explorer.

Adding the copyright symbol to a web page:

1. Click the **Start** button, and then click **Run**.

2. Type **Notepad**, and then click **OK**.

3. Type the following:

   <HTML>

   <P>&copy My Copyright page</P>

   </HTML>

4. Click **File** on the menu bar, and then click **Save As**.

5. Choose **Desktop** in the Save in: list box.

6. Type **copyright.html** in the File name: text box, and then click **Save**.

7. Close the Notepad window.

8. Double-click the **copyright.html** icon on your desktop.

9. Close Internet Explorer.

Adding the trademark symbol to a web page:

1. Click the **Start** button, and then click **Run**.

2. Type **Notepad**, and then click **OK**.

3. Type the following:

   <HTML>

   <P>&reg My trademark page</P>

   </HTML>

4. Click **File** on the menu bar, and then click **Save As**.

5. Choose the Desktop from the Save in listbox.

1

6. Type **trademark.html** in the File name: text box, and then click **Save**.

7. Close the Notepad window.

8. Double-click the **trademark.html** icon on your desktop.

9. Close Internet Explorer.

Certification Objectives:

Objectives for the i–Net+ exam:

➤ Use different types of search indexes—static index/site map, keyword index, full and text index.

➤ Identify key factors relating to legal and regulatory considerations when planning e-business solutions.

Review Questions

1. The '+' operator requires a specific search criteria to appear twice in every result. True or False?

2. An invention can be protected by a copyright. True or False?

3. A symbol can be registered as a trademark. True or False?

4. The operators that can be used to restrict searches may vary depending on the search engine. True or False?

5. The '–' operator is used to exclude specific content from search results. True or False?

6. Clint would like to search the Internet for all web pages that contain the word "Microsoft" and the name "Bill Gates". Using the search operators that you learned in this activity, write the syntax that Clint must use on the line below.

_____

LAB 1.4 RESEARCHING LOCAL INTERNET SERVICE PROVIDERS (ISPS)

Objectives

The objective of this lab is to explore the many services that can be provided by an Internet Service Provider (ISP). An ISP is a business that provides individuals and companies with access to the Internet. Typically, an ISP might offer additional features such e-mail addresses, web site space, user training, and free installation to entice prospective customers. These services make the difference between a slow and high-speed Internet connection.

To effectively do this lab, you should know the following:

➤ A digital subscriber line (DSL) is a telephone line that carries digital data from end to end, and which can be leased from the phone company for individual use. DSL lines are rated 1.5 Mbps, about 50 times faster than regular phone lines.

➤ An Integrated Services Digital Network (ISDN) line is a digital telephone line that can carry data at about five times the speed of regular phone lines. Two channels (phone numbers) share a single pair of wires.

➤ A satellite Internet connection typically requires a satellite dish and a modem. The satellite dish provides fast download speeds, which interact directly with a computer's network interface card (NIC); the modem is used to send data to the Internet.

➤ A cable modem is technology that uses cable TV lines for data transmission. This transmission requires a modem at each end. From the modem, a network cable connects to an NIC in the user's PC.

After completing this lab, you will be able to describe and compare each of the following services:

➤ Dial-up account (telephone modem connection)

➤ Digital subscriber line (DSL)

➤ Cable modem

➤ Satellite

➤ Integrated Service Digital Network (ISDN)

Materials Required

This lab will require the following:

➤ A phone book and a telephone

```
Estimated completion time: 1 hour
```

ACTIVITY

ISPs can offer a variety of services. Table 1-1 lists the different services and characteristics that might define an ISP.

1

Table 1-1   Data transmission technologies for personal and small business use

Technology	Access Method	Attainable Speeds	Current Users in U.S.	Comments
Regular phone line	Dial-up	56 Kbps	20 million	POTS—"Plain old telephone service"
DSL	Direct connect	1.5 Mbps downstream and 384 Kbps upstream	1 million	Requires a leased line from phone company
Cable modem	Direct connect	Varies up to 5 Mbps	500,000	Available through cable companies
Satellite	Direct connect	400 Kbps	NA	Only works down-stream. Upstream transmission requires a dial-up.
ISDN	Dial-up	128 Kbps	3.2 million	Requires a leased line from phone company

Contact five ISPs and research their services. Then answer the following questions.

Internet Service Provider (ISP) #1:

1. Write the name of the ISP.

   _____

2. Write the monthly charge for each of the services that the ISP offers. Be sure to find out all account features and requirements. For example, you need to know the number of e-mail addresses given with each account type, the expected connection speed, and the megabytes of web space provided.

   Dial-up account (telephone modem connection):

   _____
   _____
   _____

   DSL:

   _____
   _____
   _____

   Cable modem:

   _____
   _____
   _____

Satellite:

_____

_____

_____

ISDN:

_____

_____

_____

Internet Service Provider (ISP) #2:

1. Write the name of the ISP.

_____

2. Write the monthly charge for each of the services that the ISP offers. Be sure to find out all account features and requirements. For example, you need to know the number of e-mail addresses given with each account type, the expected connection speed, and the megabytes of web space provided.

Dial-up account (telephone modem connection):

_____

_____

_____

DSL:

_____

_____

_____

Cable modem:

_____

_____

_____

Satellite:

_____

_____

_____

ISDN:

_____

_____

_____

Internet Service Provider (ISP) #3

1. Write the name of the ISP.

   _____

2. Write the monthly charge for each of the services that the ISP offers. Be sure to find out all account features and requirements. For example, you need to know the number of e-mail addresses given with each account type, the expected connection speed, and the megabytes of web space provided.

   Dial-up account (telephone modem connection):

   _____

   _____

   _____

   DSL:

   _____

   _____

   _____

   Cable modem:

   _____

   _____

   _____

   Satellite:

   _____

   _____

   _____

   ISDN:

   _____

   _____

   _____

Internet Service Provider (ISP) #4

1. Write the name of the ISP.

   _____

2. Write the monthly charge for each of the services that the ISP offers. Be sure to find out all account features and requirements. For example, you need to know the number of e-mail addresses given with each account type, the expected connection speed, and the megabytes of web space provided.

Dial-up account (telephone modem connection):

_____

_____

_____

DSL:

_____

_____

_____

Cable modem:

_____

_____

_____

Satellite:

_____

_____

_____

ISDN:

_____

_____

_____

Internet Service Provider (ISP) #5

1. Write the name of the ISP.

_____

2. Write the monthly charge for each of the services that the ISP offers. Be sure to find out all account features and requirements. For example, you need to know the number of e-mail addresses given with each account type, the expected connection speed, and the megabytes of web space provided.

Dial-up account (telephone modem connection):

_____

_____

_____

DSL:

_____

_____

_____

Cable modem:

_____

_____

_____

Satellite:

_____

_____

_____

ISDN:

_____

_____

_____

Certification Objectives:

Objectives for the i–Net+ exam:

➤ Identify the issues that affect Internet site functionality.

➤ Understand and be able to describe the infrastructure needed to support an Internet client.

➤ Create a logic diagram of Internet components from the client to the server.

➤ Describe various hardware and software connection devices and when to use them.

Review Questions

1. An ISDN connection using both channels is faster than a 56 K dial–up connection. True or False?

2. Satellite solutions are always faster than DSL, cable modems, and ISDN. True or False?

3. ISDN is typically more expensive than DSL. True or False?

4. Lab Technology is a small business with 15 employees. Which of the five ISPs that you researched offers the best small business Internet connectivity solution? Explain your answer.

_____

_____

_____

_____

_____

5. If Peggy would like to purchase an Internet account to do streaming video web development (which requires at least 100 Kbps), which ISP and type of account would you recommend that she purchase, and why?

_____

_____

_____

_____

_____

6. If Christine would like to purchase an Internet account to use for e-mail correspondence and some light web browsing, which ISP and type of account would you recommend that she purchase, and why?

_____

_____

_____

_____

_____

_____

BUILD YOUR OWN WEB SITE

Labs included in this chapter

➤ Lab 2.1 Creating and Publishing a Web Page Using HTML

➤ Lab 2.2 Adding Customized Fonts, Graphics, and Links

➤ Lab 2.3 Adding Tables and Forms

➤ Lab 2.4 Learning About Microsoft FrontPage and Cascading Style Sheets

i-Net+ Exam Objectives	
Objective	Lab
Create HTML pages.	2.1, 2.2, 2.3, 2.4
Identify when to use various multimedia image file formats.	2.2

Lab 2.1 Creating and Publishing a Web Page Using HTML

Objectives

The objective of this lab is to create and publish an HTML web page. Before beginning, you need to know the following facts:

➤ A "tag" is an element of HTML that is interpreted by a web browser as a command to be followed, rather than text to be displayed. For example, the title tag, will inform the web browser that the information typed between the opening tag <TITLE> and the closing tag </TITLE> is the title of the web page.

➤ Your computer maintains a list of file extensions, the last three letters of a file's name, and will choose an application to open a file based on the file extension. For example, if you were to rename index.html to index.txt, your computer would use the program associated with the .txt file extension to open the index.txt file.

➤ In its simplest form, publishing a web page is the process of making a file available via a URL on a web server. You can publish a web page by simply sending it to your assigned personal web directory on a web server.

➤ An index page is the page that a web server will look for in a particular directory if no other specific web page or program is specified in the URL requested. For example, in the URL *http://www.course.com*, there no specific web page specified, so the web server will locate the index page and display that to the user.

➤ The term web host refers to a web server, which is a computer that runs a web server application and stores web site files for access via URL.

After completing this lab you will be able to:

➤ Create a web page using Notepad

➤ Publish a web page

➤ Use a web browser to test a published web page

Materials Required

This lab will require the following:

➤ Windows 9x

➤ A lab workgroup size of 2–4 students

➤ One web server

➤ Microsoft Internet Explorer 5 or later on each lab computer

➤ One directory for each student on an intranet or Internet Web server

➤ Students must be able to map a network drive to their assigned share on the web server and be provided the UNC path to connect.

➤ Student must also be provided the URL to view their personal web directory.

➤ The web server must be configured to use the name "index.html" and the index page for each student's personal web directory.

Estimated completion time: **30 minutes**

ACTIVITY

Creating a web page using Notepad:

1. Click the **Start** button, and then click **Run**.

2. Type **Notepad**, and then click the **OK** button.

3. In Notepad, type **<HTML>**. This is an opening tag used to tell your computer (web browser) what type of information to expect next. Of course, in this case, it means that the following code will be in HTML format.

4. Press **Enter** twice.

5. Type **</HTML>**, and then press the **Enter** key.

6. Click **File** on the menu bar, and then click **Save As**.

7. Click the **Save in:** drop-down arrow, and then click **Desktop**.

8. In the File Name: text box, type **index.html**.

9. Click the **Save** button. You have now created a blank web page on your desktop named index.html.

10. Click **File** on the menu bar, and then click **Exit**.

Viewing index.html:

1. Double-click the **index.html** icon, which is on your desktop.

2. Notice that the Address bar now contains a path to the file rather than a URL beginning with "http://".

3. On the line provided, describe what, if anything, is displayed in your web browser window.

_____

4. Explain the results from Step 3. Why did your web browser display or not display anything in the browser window?

_____

5. Close Internet Explorer.

Adding a title to index.html:

1. Click the **Start** button, and then click **Run**.

2. Type **Notepad**, and then click the **OK** button.

3. Click **File** on the menu bar, and then click **Open**. Select **Desktop** in the Look in: list box, if necessary.

4. Click the **Files of Type:** drop-down arrow, and then click **All Files**.

5. Double-click the **index.html** icon.

6. In the Notepad window, use the down arrow on your keyboard to move the insertion point to the second line, which is the line between the two html tags.

7. Type **<TITLE>This is the title of my index page</TITLE>**. The title tag is used to title your web page. Internet Explorer will display the information found between the two title tags in the blue title bar of the browser.

8. Click **File** on the menu bar, and then click **Save**. This will save the changes you have made to index.html.

9. Click **File** on the menu bar, and then click **Exit**.

10. Double-click the **index.html** icon, which is on your desktop.

11. On the line provided, describe where Internet Explorer displays the title.

_____

12. Close Internet Explorer.

Adding text to index.html:

1. Click the **Start** button, and then click **Run**.

2. Type **Notepad**, and then click the **OK** button.

3. Click **File** on the menu bar, and then click **Open**. Select **Desktop** in the Look in: list box, if necessary.

4. Click the **Files of Type:** drop-down arrow, and then click **All Files**.

5. Double-click the **index.html** icon.

6. In the Notepad window, use the down arrow on your keyboard to move the insertion point down to the third line, which should be blank.

7. Type **<HEAD>This is the Header</HEAD>**, and press **Enter**.

8. Click **File** on the menu bar, and then click **Save**.

9. Exit Notepad.

10. Click **File** on the menu bar, and then click **Exit**.

11. Open index.html using Internet Explorer. Double-click the **index.html** icon, which is on your desktop.

12. On the line provided, describe where Internet Explorer displays the header.

_____

13. Close Internet Explorer.

Publishing index.html on a web server:

1. Right-click the **Network Neighborhood** icon on your desktop, and then click **Map Network Drive**.

2. In the path text box, type the UNC path provided by your instructor.

3. Click **OK**.

4. After your computer has made the network connection, a window will open, showing the contents of the directory. Click and hold down the left mouse button on top of the index.html icon found on your desktop.

5. Drag the icon into the network drive window. Then release the mouse button. You have successfully copied index.html to the network drive window if the icon now appears both in the window and on your desktop.

6. Close the network drive window.

7. Right-click the **Network Neighborhood** icon on your desktop, and then click **Disconnect Network Drive**.

8. Double-click the network drive connected to your personal web directory assigned by your instructor.

Viewing the published web page:

1. Open Internet Explorer using the icon on your desktop.

2. On the line provided, write the URL to your personal web directory.

   _____

3. In the Address bar, type the URL to your personal directory on the web server, and then press **Enter**.

4. On the line provided, describe what, if anything, is displayed in your web browser window.

   _____

5. Explain the results from Step 4. Why did your web browser display or not display anything in the browser window?

   _____

6. Close Internet Explorer.

Certification Objectives:

Objectives for the i-Net+ exam:

➤ Create HTML pages.

Review Questions

1. Every web page must contain both an open and close html tag. True or False?

2. The text between the arrows of a tag (<...>) will always be displayed in the browser window. True or False?

3. Debug the following line of HTML code. Rewrite the entire line of code, in the correct format, on the line provided.

   ```
   <HEAD> The World OF Computers! <HEAD>
   ```

   _____

4. Debug the following line of HTML code. Rewrite the entire line of code, in the correct format, on the line provided.

   ```
   </TITLE> The World OF Computers Home page! <TITLE>
   ```

   _____

5. Determine if the following code forms a valid web page. If anything is missing, write it on the line provided; otherwise, write "Web page is valid."

   ```
   <HTML>

   <TITLE> My personal WEB page</TITLE>

   <HEAD> The World OF Computers! </HEAD>
   ```

   _____

6. On the lines provided, describe, in your own words, what it means to "publish" a web document.

   _____

   _____

   _____

   _____

   _____

LAB 2.2 ADDING CUSTOMIZED FONTS, GRAPHICS, AND LINKS

Objectives

You can customize and enhance a web page using a variety of fonts, graphics, and links. To effectively do so, you need to know the following facts:

➤ A Joint Photographic Experts Groups (JPEG) file is a type of compressed file commonly used to hold photographs. The file can contain up to 1.6 million colors or be grayscale and does not allow a transparent background.

➤ A Graphic Interchange Format (GIF) file is probably the most popular graphics file on the Web. GIF files are bit-mapped files that most web browsers and other software can easily read.

➤ A Portable Network Graphics (PNG) file is a graphics file used for clip art that supports a transparent background, but that does not support animated clip art.

➤ A Portable Document Format (PDF) file is a proprietary file type from Adobe Systems. PDF files are designed to retain the original formatting and yet be easy for anyone to view and print. They are a popular way to deliver software documentation electronically, especially for software that is available via download.

➤ A Tagged Image File Format (TIFF) file is popular for desktop publishing applications. TIFF files are often used for photographs and screen captures as well as other graphics. They are bit-mapped images that can use either lossless or lossy compression and offer strong support for color. TIFF files can be rather large and are not supported by most browsers without a plug-in, so they are not as popular on the Web as other file types.

➤ A Bit-Mapped (BMP) file is an older type of graphic file that doesn't support high resolution, animation, interlacing or compression. Because BMP files are not compressed, they are not recommended for the Web, but the format has remained popular because it is easy to use.

After completing the following lab, you will be able to:

➤ Format and customize web page text using the paragraph and bold tags

➤ Link your web page to a classmate's web page using a hyperlink

➤ Add a graphic to a web page

Materials Required

This lab will require the following:

➤ Windows 9x

➤ A lab workgroup size of 2–4 students

➤ One web server

➤ Microsoft Internet Explorer 5 or later on each lab computer.

➤ The index.html web page from Lab 3.2

➤ A shortcut to Internet Explorer on the desktop of each computer

➤ Each lab computer must have one graphic on the desktop named "Webgraphic.jpg." Students will publish this graphic on the web server. This graphic can be anything that is readily available to the instructor.

➤ Students must be able to map a network drive to their assigned share on the web server, and be provided the UNC path to connect. Student must also be provided the URL to view their personal web directory.

➤ The web server must be configured to use the name "index.html" and the index page for each student's personal web directory.

Estimated completion time: **30 minutes**

ACTIVITY

Customizing index.html:

1. Click the **Start** button, and then click **Run**.

2. Type **Notepad**, and then click the **OK** button.

3. Click **File** on the menu bar, and then click **Open**. Select **Desktop** in the Look in: list box, if necessary.

4. Click the **Files of Type:** drop-down arrow, and then click **All Files**.

5. Double-click **index.html**.

6. In the Notepad window, add the following text using the paragraph and bold tags. This text must be added anywhere between the beginning and ending HTML tags, but NOT between any other tags.

   `<P>This sentence formatted using a paragraph tag and this word is <B>bold</B></P>`

7. When you have finished, save **index.html** and publish it to your personal web directory. If you need help publishing your web page, refer to Lab 2.1.

8. Open Internet Explorer by double-clicking the **Internet Explorer** icon on your desktop, and then type the URL to your personal web directory.

9. Close Internet Explorer.

Adding a graphic to index.html:

1. Click the **Start** button, and then click **Run**.

2. Type **Notepad**, and then click the **OK** button.

3. Click **File** on the menu bar, and then click **Open**.

4. Click the **Files of Type:** drop-down arrow, and then click **All Files**.

5. Double-click **index.html**.

6. Move the insertion point to a position in the index.html file where you would like to add a graphic.

7. Type **<IMG SRC="./Webgraphic.jpg">**, and then press **Enter**.

8. Save the change to index.html.

9. Publish both index.html *and* Webgraphic.jpg to your personal web directory.

2

10. Open Internet Explorer by double-clicking the **Internet Explorer** icon found on your desktop, and then type the URL to your personal web directory.

11. Close Internet Explorer.

12. Close all open windows when you have finished.

Adding a link to index.html:

1. Click the **Start** button, and then click **Run**.

2. Type **Notepad**, and then click the **OK** button.

3. Click **File** on the menu bar, and then click **Open**.

4. Click the **Files of Type:** drop-down arrow, and then click **All Files**.

5. Double-click **index.html**.

6. Move the insertion point to a position in the index.html file where you would like to add a link.

7. Type **<A HREF=http://"www.microsoft.com">The Microsoft Web Site </A>**, and then press **Enter**.

8. Save the change to index.html and publish it to your personal directory.

9. Open Internet Explorer by double-clicking the **Internet Explorer** icon on your desktop, and then type the URL to your personal web directory.

10. On the line provided, describe how the link is displayed on your web site.

_____

11. Using the same HREF tag, create links on your index.html page that reference two of your classmates' URLs.

12. Close Internet Explorer and all open windows when you have finished.

Certification Objectives:

Objectives for the i-Net+ exam:

➤ Create HTML pages

➤ Identify when to use various image multimedia file formats

Review Questions

1. This HTML tag is used to add a graphic to a web page: <IMG SCREEN="file name">. True or False?

2. An HREF tag is also called a link. True or False?

3. The PDF format is proprietary and was developed by Adobe. True or False?

4. Only GIF and PNG graphic files can be posted to a web page. True or False?

5. An HREF tag can be used to link a web page to any other web page on the Internet. True or False?

6. On the lines provided describe the solution to the stated problem. When you click a link, the following error message is displayed: Error Code 404 File not found.

_____

_____

_____

_____

_____

LAB 2.3 ADDING TABLES AND FORMS

Objectives

A form is an HTML element that allows a web page to collect data from the user and send it back to the web server or an e-mail recipient. The goal of this lab is to create tables and forms for web documents. A form is a way of requesting data from a user. Forms vary in complexity; a simple form will collect the data from a user and e-mail it to a specified e-mail address. You will use the tags in Table 2-1 as you work through this lab.

Table 2-1   Tags to create tables in HTML

Tag	Description
<TABLE> </TABLE>	Beginning and end of the table
<TR> </TR>	Beginning and end of one row of a table
<TD> </TD>	Beginning and end of one cell in one row of a table
<CAPTION> </CAPTION>	Title of the table written above the table (optional tag)
<TH> </TH>	Column heading over one column in a table (optional table)

After completing this lab, you will be able to:

➤ Add a table to your web page

➤ Create a web form

Materials Required

This lab will require the following:

➤ Windows 9x

➤ A lab workgroup size of 2–4 students

➤ One web server

> ➤ Microsoft Internet Explorer 5 or later installed on each lab computer

> ➤ A shortcut to Internet Explorer on the desktop of each computer

> ➤ Students must be able to map a network drive to their assigned share on the web server and be provided the UNC path to connect. Students must also be provided the URLs to view their personal web directories.

> ➤ The web server must be configured to use the name "index.html" and the index page for each student's personal web directory.

Estimated completion time: **60 minutes**

ACTIVITY

Adding a table to index.html:

1. Click the **Start** button, and then click **Run**.

2. Type **Notepad**, and then click the **OK** button.

3. Click **File** on the menu bar, and then click **Open**. Select **Desktop** in the Look in: list box, if necessary.

4. Click the **Files of Type:** drop-down arrow, and then click **All Files**.

5. Double-click **index.html**.

6. Move the insertion point to a position in the index.html file to where you would like to add a table.

7. Type **<TABLE BORDER="1">**, and then press **Enter**.

8. Type **<CAPTION> Multiplication Tables</CAPTION>**, and press **Enter**.

9. To begin the first row of the table, type **<TR>**, and then press **Enter**.

10. Type **<TH>Multiple </TH>**, and then press **Enter**.

11. Type **<TH>X 1 </TH>**, and then press **Enter**.

12. Type **<TH>X 2 </TH>**, and then press **Enter**.

13. Type **<TH>X 3 </TH>**, and then press **Enter**.

14. To end the first row of the table, type **</TR>**, and then press **Enter**.

15. Press **Enter** and type **<TR>** to begin a new row.

16. Type **<TD>1 </TD>**, and then press **Enter**.

17. Type **<TD>1</TD>**, and then press **Enter**.

18. Type **<TD>2 </TD>** and then press **Enter**.

19. Type **<TD>3 </TD>**, and then press **Enter**.

20. To end the first row of the table, type **</TR>** and then press **Enter**.

21. Press **Enter**, and type **<TR>** to begin a new row. The second row in the table uses the exact same HTML syntax, so you need only change the data.

22. Type **<TD>2 </TD>**, and then press **Enter**.

23. Type **<TD>2 </TD>**, and then press **Enter**.

24. Type **<TD>4 </TD>**, and then press **Enter**.

25. Type **<TD>6 </TD>**, and then press **Enter**.

26. To end the second row of the table, type **</TR>** and then press **Enter**.

27. Type **</TABLE>** to end the table. When you have finished the HTML code for your table, it should resemble the code in Figure 2-1.

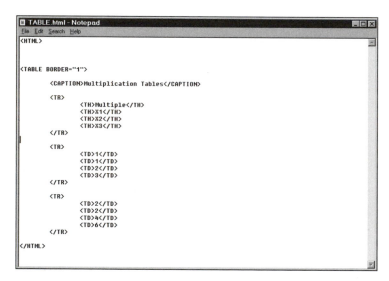

Figure 2-1   Sample HTML code for a multiplication table

28. Save the change to index.html and publish it to your personal directory.

Creating a form:

1. Click the **Start** button, and then click **Run**.

2. Type **Notepad**, and then click the **OK** button.

3. Click **File** on the menu bar, and then click **Open**. Select **Desktop** in the Look in: list box, if necessary.

4. Click the **Files of Type:** drop-down arrow, and then click **All Files**.

5. Double-click **index.html**.

6. Move the insertion point to a position in the index.html file to where you would like to add a form.

7. Type **<FORM METHOD="POST" ACTION="mailto:myemail@address.com">**, where *myemail@address.com* is your e-mail address. Press **Enter**.

8. Type **<P> Enter Your Name Here: <INPUT TYPE="text" NAME="Customer_Name">
, and then press **Enter.

9. Type **Enter Your Company Name Here: <INPUT TYPE="text" NAME="Company_Name">
 </P>**, and then press **Enter**.

10. Type **<INPUT TYPE="submit" VALUE="Send">**, and then press **Enter**.

11. Type **</FORM>**, and then press **Enter**.

12. Save the change to index.html and publish it to your personal directory. When you have finished, the HTML code for your form should resemble the code in Figure 2-2.

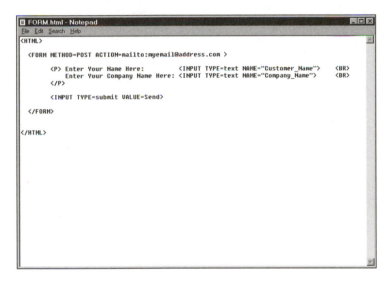

Figure 2-2   Sample HTML code for a form

13. Add two new text fields to the form named City and Country. Save the changes when you are finished.

14. On the lines provided, write the code that you used to add the City and Country text fields to your form.

_____

_____

_____

_____

_____

Certification Objectives

Objectives for the i–Net+ exam:

➤ Create HTML pages.

Review Questions

1. The <TITLE> tag is used to write the title of a table to a web document. True or False?

2. <INPUT TYPE="Submit" VALUE="temp"> will create a button named Submit in a web document. True or False?

3. Data can be submitted from a form to a program by changing the form's "ACTION". True or False?

4. The <TH> tag is used to title a HTML table column. True or False?

5. On the lines provided write the complete HTML code for a table contain two rows and two columns. (*Hint:* Don't forget the <HTML> tags!)

_____

_____

_____

_____

_____

_____

_____

_____

_____

6. On the lines provided, write the complete HTML code for a single web page that contains one form with five text fields. The form's ACTION should be to e-mail you the results. (*Hint:* Don't forget the <HTML> tags!)

_____

_____

_____

_____

_____

_____

_____

_____

LAB 2.4 LEARNING ABOUT MICROSOFT FRONTPAGE AND CASCADING STYLE SHEETS

Objectives

Think of a cascading style sheet as a template. Whatever you specify in a style sheet can be applied to one or more web documents. To apply a style sheet to a web document, you must first link the web document to the style sheet.

A Cascading Style Sheet (CSS) is a specification for style sheets, developed by the World Wide Web Consortium, which defines how a style sheet controls the formatting of an HTML document. A style sheet is a text file with a .css file extension that contains rules about how a browser should display a web page. A style sheet can include information such as what font to use when displaying text, what background color to use, or what margins to use. A style sheet is linked to an HTML document and controls the formatting of that document.

CSSs allow a web developer to manipulate the look and feel of many web pages by simply changing one file. This ability makes style sheets extremely powerful. Style sheets should be used as often as possible, especially if you expect a web site to grow or already have numerous web pages to manage.

During the following lab activities, you will be switching between three different views. In the FrontPage window, near the bottom, you will see three tabs: Normal, HTML, and Preview. On the Normal tab, the default view, you can design a web document and FrontPage will write the HTML code for you. The HTML tab will allow you to view and modify the HTML code generated by FrontPage. The Preview tab will allow you to preview a web document before you publish it to a web site.

After completing this lab, you will be able to:

➤ Create a style sheet using Microsoft FrontPage

➤ Apply a style sheet to a standard HTML web page

➤ Describe how a style sheet affects a web page

➤ Determine when it would be appropriate to use a style sheet

Materials Required

This lab will require the following:

➤ Windows 9x

➤ A lab workgroup size of 2–4 students

> ➤ One web server
> ➤ Microsoft Internet Explorer 5 or later installed on each lab computer
> ➤ Microsoft FrontPage 2000
> ➤ A web server running Microsoft FrontPage Sever Extension 2000
> ➤ A shortcut to Internet Explorer on the desktop of each computer
> ➤ Students must be able to map a network drive to their assigned share on the web server, and be provided the UNC path to connect. Students must also be provided the URL to view their personal web directory. Each student's personal web share must also be a FrontPage 2000 web.
> ➤ The web server must be configured to use the name "index.html" and the index page for each student's personal web directory.
> ➤ Each lab computer must have a shortcut to Microsoft FrontPage 2000 on the desktop.

Estimated completion time: **45 minutes**

ACTIVITY

Connecting to your FrontPage web:

1. Double-click the **Microsoft FrontPage** icon found on your desktop.
2. Click **File** on the menu bar, and then click **Open Web**.
3. In the Folder name: text box, type the web address to your personal FrontPage web. Your instructor will provide the correct address to your personal web share. Click **Open**.
4. If you are prompted for a user name and password, type in your logon information (provided by your instructor), and then click **OK**.
5. If you were required to enter a user name and password, click **OK** again.

Creating a FrontPage CSS:

1. Click **File** on the menu bar, click **New**, and then click **Page**.
2. Click the **Style Sheets** tab and double-click **Normal Style Sheet**.
3. Click **Format** on the menu bar, and then click **Style**.
4. In the Style dialog box, scroll down, and then click **h1**.
5. Click the **Modify** button.
6. Click the **Format** button, and then click **Font**.
7. Click **Arial Black**, click **Italic**, and then click **OK**.

8. Click **OK**. Notice in the Style dialog box that h1 now appears in the user-defined style list.

9. Click **OK**.

10. Click **File** on the menu bar, and then click **Save As**.

11. Type **MyStyles**, and then click **Save**.

Creating an index page for your FrontPage web:

1. Click **File**, click **New**, and then click **Page**.

2. On the General tab, double-click **Normal Page**.

3. Click **Format** on the menu bar, and then click **Font**.

4. In the Size: list box, click **4 (14 pts)**, and then click **OK**.

5. There are three list boxes near the top of the FrontPage window. Select the leftmost list box, and then click **Heading 1**. This will tell FrontPage that the next line of type should be created using the <H1> HTML tag rather than a <P> paragraph HTML tag.

6. Select the rightmost list box, and then click **4 (14 pt)**. This will tell FrontPage that the next line of type should be created using a 14-point font.

7. On the blank web page, type **This is Heading 1 using 14 point font**.

8. Near the bottom of the FrontPage window, click the HTML tab. Find the text "This is Heading 1 using 14 point font". If the list boxes were set as described in Steps 6 and 7, the sentence you typed will appear like this: <H1><FONT SIZE="4">This is Heading 1 using 14 point font</FONT></H1>.

9. Click the **Preview** tab to preview the web page.

10. Click **File** on the menu bar, and then click **Save As**.

11. Type **index.html**, and then click **Save**.

Applying MyStyles.css to index.html:

1. With the index.html Web page still open, click the **Normal** tab.

2. Click **Format**, and then click **Style Sheet Links**.

3. Click **Add**, and double-click **MyStyles.css**.

4. Click the **Selected Page(s)** button, and then click **OK**.

5. Click the **Preview** tab.

6. On the lines provided, describe the changes and explain how the style sheet affected index.html.

_____

_____

_____

_____

7. Click the **HTML** tab.

8. Notice the HTML code that FrontPage generated to apply the MyStyles.css to the index.html web document.

9. Click **File**, and then click **Save**.

10. Click **File**, and then click **Exit**.

Certification Objectives:

Objectives for the i-Net+ exam:

➤ Create HTML pages

Review Questions

1. A web developer can apply one change to multiple web documents using a style sheet. True or False?

2. Style sheets are web pages that save additional information about fonts. True or False?

3. A style sheet is a web page. True or False?

4. The World Wide Web Consortium defined the specifications for css files. True or False?

5. Using style sheets, a company could apply a standardized look and feel to all of their web documents. True or False?

6. You have an existing style sheet that has been applied to two web documents. You have been asked to italicize the <H6> HTML tag in both web documents and create a third web document with the same formatting as the existing two documents. On the lines provided, answer the following questions.

   a. Where should you modify the <H6> formatting?

   b. How can you easily guarantee that the new web document will have the same formatting as the existing two web documents?

_____

_____

_____

_____

_____

HOW CLIENTS AND SERVERS WORK TOGETHER

Labs included in this chapter

➤ Lab 3.1 Using and Understanding E-Mail Communication

➤ Lab 3.2 Using and Understanding FTP

➤ Lab 3.3 Using and Understanding Telnet and Newsgroups

➤ Lab 3.4 Server Research Project

➤ Lab 3.5 Installing the Apache Web Server

---

i-Net+ Exam Objectives	
Objective	**Lab**
Understand and be able to describe the infrastructure needed to support an Internet client.	3.1
Use/configure Web browsers and other Internet/intranet clients, and be able to describe their use to others.	3.1, 3.2, 3.3
Understand and be able to describe the concept of caching and its implications.	3.4
Identify problems with Internet connectivity from source to destination for various types of servers.	3.4
Understand how various protocols or services apply to the function of their corresponding server, such as a mail server, a web server or a file transfer server.	3.4
Understand and be able to describe the capabilities of application server providers.	3.4
Assist in the administration of Internet/intranet sites.	3.5
Test pre-production Web and e-commerce servers.	3.5

Lab 3.1 Using and Understanding E-Mail Communication

Objectives

E-mail is more than clicking the Send button and waiting for a reply. There are many elements that play a part to ensure a satisfactory e-mail exchange:

➤ **Helper application:** An application used by e-mail client software to interpret and display attachments.

➤ **IMAP4 (Internet Message Access Protocol):** An e-mail protocol that has more functionality than its predecessor, POP. IMAP can archive messages in folders on the e-mail sever and can allow the user to choose to not download attachments to files.

➤ **List server:** Software, running on a server, that maintains and manages a list of e-mail addresses and messages to multiple addresses on the list.

➤ **MAPI:** A specification that allows an application to interact with an e-mail client to send and receive e-mail.

➤ **POP3:** POP (Post Office Protocol) version 3 is a protocol used by an e-mail server and client when the client requests to download e-mail messages. POP is slowly becoming outdated because of the IMAP protocol, but is still the most prevalent on the Internet.

➤ **SMTP:** SMTP (simple mail transfer protocol) is a protocol used by e-mail clients and servers to send e-mail messages over the Internet.

➤ **MIME (Multipurpose Internet Mail Extensions):** A protocol that allows non-text files to be attached to e-mail messages or downloaded to a web browser along with a web page. MIME identifies a file as belonging to a category and subcategory such as Image/gif. Files are encoded using a method that the SMTP protocol can handle when it processes the e-mail message.

All these elements work together. For instance, e-mail client software communicates with an e-mail server when it sends and receives e-mail. Figure 3-1 shows a user with one mail server, which both sends and receives messages for the user.

In fact, it's possible to have two e-mail severs, one for sending e-mail and the other for receiving e-mail. Figure 3-2 shows this arrangement.

The e-mail server that takes care of sending e-mail messages (using the SMTP protocol) is often referred to as the SMTP server. The e-mail server from which you collect messages that were sent to you is often referred to as the POP3 server, because it uses the POP3 protocol.

How does the e-mail client software know which SMTP and POP3 server(s) to use? When you configure your e-mail client software for the first time, you enter this information. If you are connecting to e-mail via an Internet Service Provider (ISP), the ISP will provide you with the server names and logon information required.

3

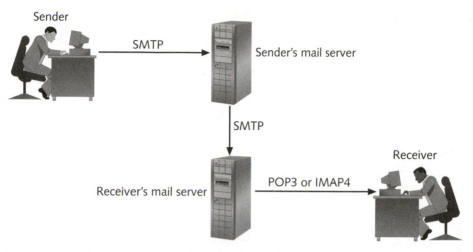

Figure 3-1 The SMTP protocol is used to send e-mail to a recipient's mail server, and POP3 or IMAP4 protocol is used to download e-mail to the client

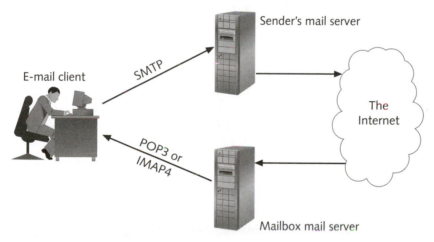

Figure 3-2 An e-mail client can use one server to send e-mail and another to receive e-mail

After completing this lab, you will be able to:

➤ Use and describe electronic messaging on the Internet

➤ Understand the most common configuration requirements and how to use them when configuring an e-mail client

Materials Required

This lab will require the following:

➤ Windows 9x

➤ A workgroup size of 2–4 students

➤ Microsoft Outlook Express 5 or later

➤ A POP3 e-mail account and the name or address of the POP3 and SMTP server(s)

Estimated completion time: **30 minutes**

ACTIVITY

Understanding electronic messaging:

1. On the line provided, write down the e-mail address provided by your instructor.

_____

2. On the line provided, write down the name or IP address of your SMTP server (outgoing mail).

_____

3. On the line provided, write down the name or IP address of your POP server (incoming mail).

_____

Configuring Outlook Express:

1. Click the **Start** button, point to **Programs**, and then click **Outlook Express**.

2. If Outlook Express has never been configured before on your lab computer, you may be prompted by a configuration wizard. Click the **Cancel** button until you can see the default Outlook Express window.

3. Click the **Tools** menu, and then click **Accounts**.

4. Click the **Mail** tab. Your screen should resemble Figure 3-3.

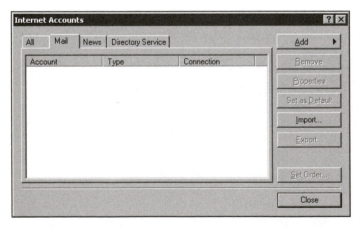

Figure 3-3   Mail tab

5. Click the **Add** button, and then click **Mail**.

6. Type your name in the Display Name text box. This name will be the common name displayed for your e-mail address.

7. Click the **Next** button.

8. Click the **I already have an e-mail address I'd like to use** button, and then type your e-mail address into the accompanying text box.

9. Click the **Next** button.

10. In the Incoming mail server text box, type the name or address for your POP3 server.

11. In the Outgoing mail server text box, type the name or address for your SMTP server.

12. Click the **Next** button.

13. In the Account Name: text box, type the logon name for your e-mail account.

14. In the Password: text box, type the password for your e-mail account.

15. Click the **Next** button.

16. Click the **Finish** button.

17. Notice that your mail server now appears on the Mail tab of the Internet Account dialog box. Click the **Close** button.

Sending and receiving e-mail messages:

1. Click the **New Mail** button in the upper-left corner of the Outlook Express window, as shown in Figure 3-4.

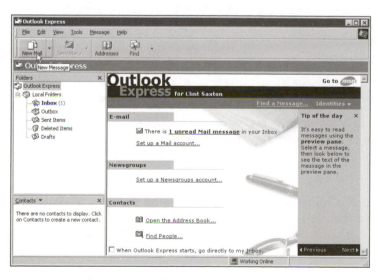

Figure 3-4   New Mail button

2. In the To: box, type your complete e-mail address. For example, you can type *yourname@domain.com*.

3. Press **Tab** twice.

4. With the insertion point in the Subject: text box, type **Test Message from myself**.

5. Press **Tab**.

6. In the body of the message, type **Hello, this is a test message**.

7. Click **Send**. This will place your test message in the Outbox. Message placed in the Outbox will be sent the next time you send and receive messages.

8. Click the **Send/Receive** button.

9. In the folder list, click your **Inbox**.

10. In the message list, double-click the message with the subject Test Message from myself.

11. Close the message by clicking the **X** in the upper-right corner of the message window.

12. Close Outlook Express by clicking the **X** in the upper-right corner of the Outlook Express window.

Certification Objectives:

Objectives for the i-Net+ exam:

➤ Understand and be able to describe the infrastructure needed to support an Internet client.

➤ Use/configure Web browsers and other Internet/intranet clients, and be able to describe their use to others.

Review Questions

1. The POP3 protocol is used to send and receive e-mail but is becoming slowly outdated because of the IMAP protocol. True or False?

2. Sometimes two separate mail servers are used for e-mail, one to send messages and one to receive messages. True or False?

3. To send and receive e-mail, you must use SMTP and POP, unless you are using the IMAP protocol. True or False?

4. The simple mail transport protocol is used on the Internet to send e-mail messages. True or False?

5. In your own words, describe the function of a helper application.

_____

_____

_____

_____

_____

6. In your own words, describe the main purpose for POP.

_____

_____

_____

_____

_____

LAB 3.2 USING AND UNDERSTANDING FTP

Objectives

The File Transfer Protocol (FTP) is used to transfer files over the Internet so that the file does not need to be converted to ASCII format before the transfer. An FTP server identifies a user on an FTP site by the user's ID. When you first log into an FTP site, the permissions that have been granted to you determine what the FTP server allows you to do. A user with the correct permissions can copy, delete, and rename files, make directories, remove directories, and view details about files and directories on the remote computer.

FTP client and server software create a session (working at the Session layer of the OSI model) between them after you are logged in. The FTP client has access to the file system on the server, as seen in Figure 3-5.

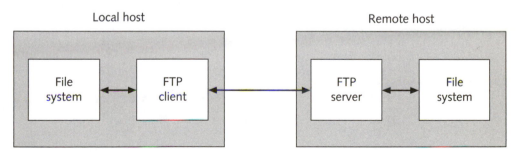

Figure 3-5 FTP client and server software have access to their individual file systems—files can be transferred in either direction

Text files stored in ASCII format are referred to as ASCII files. ASCII stands for the American Standard Code for Information Interchange. ASCII characters are 8-bit characters; each character is assigned a number from 0 to 255. An anonymous FTP site does not require a user to log in with a valid ID or password. Anonymous FTP sites are used to download files, but not used to receive uploaded files.

After completing this lab, you will be able to:

➤ Use the File Transfer Protocol (FTP) on the Internet, and describe how it is used

Materials Required

This lab will require the following:

➤ Windows 9x

➤ A lab workgroup size of 2–4 students

➤ Internet Explorer 5 or later installed on each lab computer

➤ A shortcut to Internet Explorer on the desktop of each lab computer

➤ A connection to the Internet for each computer

Estimated completion time: **45 minutes**

ACTIVITY

Connecting to an FTP site using the command line:

1. Click the **Start** button, and then click **Run**.

2. Type **command**, and then click **OK**.

3. Type **ftp ftp.microsoft.com**, and then press **Enter**.

4. Type **anonymous**, and then press **Enter**.

5. Type *youremail@address.com*, and then press **Enter**. Substitute the address shown for your own e-mail address.

Downloading a file using FTP:

1. After you have successfully logged on to the Microsoft FTP site, type **ls**, and then press **Enter**, to see a directory listing.

2. Type **cd softlib**, and then press **Enter**.

3. Type **ls**, and then press **Enter**. Notice the file named index.txt.

4. Type **get index.txt**, and then press **Enter**. This will download the index.txt file to your computer.

5. Type **bye** to disconnect the FTP session, and read any closing messages, if they appear.

6. Type **Enter** to end the command line session, and then close the FTP window.

Connecting to an FTP site using Internet Explorer:

1. Double-click the **Internet Explorer** icon found on your desktop.

2. In the Address bar, type **ftp://ftp.microsoft.com**, and then press **Enter**. If you do not specify a user ID and password, Internet Explorer will automatically log into an ftp site using the anonymous user ID.

3

Downloading a file using FTP and Internet Explorer:

1. After you have successfully logged in to the Microsoft FTP, double-click the **softlib** folder. Notice that this is the same folder from the command line activity and that it contains the same files.

2. Double-click the **index.txt** file.

3. On the line provided, describe the results and compare the difference between downloading a file using Internet Explorer and the command line.

_____

_____

_____

_____

_____

Certification Objectives:

Objectives for the i-Net+ exam:

➤ Use/configure Web browsers and other Internet/intranet clients, and be able to describe their use to others.

Review Questions

1. The ls command is used to link system files to an FTP site. True or False?

2. When you log into an anonymous FTP site, your email address is typically requested as the password. True or False?

3. If permissions have been set correctly, FTP can be used to delete files on a remote server. True or False?

4. Web developers often use FTP to publish web documents. True or False?

5. On the lines provided, write the full paths for three anonymous FTP servers that can be found on the Internet. (*Hint:* Try major computer manufacturer web sites; they often have anonymous FTP servers.)

_____

_____

_____

6. Search the Internet for three different FTP client software programs, and then write the name of each program and manufacturer on the lines provided.

_____

_____

_____

_____

_____

LAB 3.3 USING AND UNDERSTANDING TELNET AND NEWSGROUPS

Objectives

A Telnet window is a command window to a remote computer where any command can be executed, just as though the user were sitting at the computer console. Telnet is the service used to pass commands and replies between the client and the remote computer. By default, a Telnet session, which is communication between a client and a server, uses TCP port 23. Telnet was originally designed for use with UNIX computers; however, in recent years, Microsoft has developed a Widows client and server Telnet component.

In addition to the Telnet service, newsgroups are also used on the Internet. A newsgroup is a service on the Internet or private network where a group of people can post articles and responses to those articles so that information can be shared among the members of the group. Figure 3-6 depicts how a news server interacts with clients on the Internet.

Figure 3-6   Outlook Express is used as a newsgroup client—click an article to view it

A newsgroup uses the Network News Transfer Protocol (NNTP). This protocol works much like the SMTP, whereby commands are issued from the client or requesting server as character-based words with arguments following. Replies come from the news server in the form of numeric codes with descriptive text following. Table 3-1 contains an example of a sample dialog between two computers running the newsgroup service.

3

Table 3-1   Sample dialog between a newsgroup client and server

Computer	Information Transmitted	Description
Server:	--	Listening on port 119
Client:	Requests session with news.myserver.com port 119	TCP request for connection to server at port 119
Server:	200 news.myserver.com ready	Connection confirmed.
Client:	LIST	What are your current newsgroups?
Server:	215	My list follows.
Server:	rec.sport.skating.ice.recreational10 490 500 rec.sport.skating.ice.figure 5 200 205 (others follow)	For this newsgroup, there are 10 articles, numbers 490-500. For this newsgroup, there are 5 articles, numbers 200-205.
Client:	GROUP rec.sport.skating.ice.figure	I'm interested in this group.
Server:	211 5 200 205 rec.sport.skating.ice.figure	Here's what I have about that group.
Client:	HEAD 200	Send me the header information for article 200.
Server:	221 200 (header follows)	Here is the header for article 200.
Client:	ARTICLE 200	Send me the entire article, header and body.
Server:	220 200 (article follows)	Here it is.
Client:	QUIT	That's all. I'm done.
Server:	205	Goodbye.

After completing this lab, you will be able to:

➤ Use and describe Telnet

➤ Configure Outlook Express to connect to a newsgroup server

➤ Download available newsgroups from a newsgroup server

Materials Required

This lab will require the following:

➤ Windows 9x

➤ A lab workgroup size of 2–4 students

➤ Microsoft Outlook Express 5 installed on each lab computer

➤ A shortcut to Outlook Express on the desktop of each computer

➤ Each lab computer must have access to a server that will allow Telnet login.

➤ Each lab computer must have access to a newsgroup server.

➤ The instructor must provide activity steps so that the exercise can be customized for the classroom environment. The activity steps must include the use of three different commands using Telnet.

Estimated completion time: **30 minutes**

ACTIVITY

Connecting to a server using Telnet:

1. Click **Start**, and then click **Run**.

2. Type **telnet** *servername*, where *servername* is the server name provided by your instructor, and click **OK**.

3. In the Telnet window, type the user ID provided by your instructor, and press **Enter**. Note that if you mistype the ID, you cannot use the Backspace key. You must instead close the Telnet window and reconnect.

4. Type the password, and then press **Enter**.

5. After you have logged in, complete the instructions provided by your instructor.

6. Type **exit** to disconnect the Telnet session.

7. Close the Telnet window.

Configuring Outlook Express to download newsgroups:

1. Double-click the **Outlook Express** icon found on your desktop.

2. If Outlook Express has never been configured before on your lab computer, you may be prompted by a configuration wizard. Click the **Cancel** button until you can see the default Outlook Express window.

3. Click the **Tools** menu, and then click **Accounts**.

4. Click the **News** tab.

5. Click **Add**, and then click **News**.

6. Type your name in the Display Name text box. This name will be the common name displayed for your e-mail address.

7. Click **Next**.

8. Type your e-mail address in the E-mail address text box, and then click **Next**.

9. In the News (NTTP) server text box, type the name or address for your news server (provided by your instructor).

10. Click **Next**.

11. Click **Finish**, and then click **OK**.

12. Click **Yes** when prompted to download a newsgroup.

Certification Objectives:

Objectives for the i–Net+ exam:

➤ Use/configure Web browsers and other Internet/intranet clients, and be able to describe their use to others.

➤ Identify problems with Internet connectivity from source to destination for various types of servers.

➤ Understand how various protocols or services apply to the function of their corresponding server, such as a mail server, a web server, or a file transfer server.

Review Questions

1. Telnet is a service used to transfer files across networks. True or False?

2. Telnet was originally developed for use with Windows computers. True or False?

3. If a server is configured correctly, remote administration can be performed via a Telnet window. True or False?

4. Telnet uses TCP port 23 by default. True or False?

5. Newsgroup servers listen on TCP port 119. True or False?

6. List three commands that can be executed in a Telnet window.

_____

_____

_____

_____

_____

LAB 3.4 SERVER RESEARCH PROJECT

Objectives

The goal of this lab activity is to provide you with a general overview of the many different types of server software available.

After completing this lab, you will be able to:

➤ Describe different types of server software available and discuss how they can be used in a business environment

➤ Discuss the price range and manufacturers of many different types of server software

Materials Required

This lab will require the following:

➤ Access to the Internet

Estimated completion time: **1 hour**

ACTIVITY

Using the Internet, research the characteristics of one certificate server software product:

1. Name of the product: _____

2. Manufacturer: _____

3. Retail price: _____

4. Summarize the product's purpose and functionality:

_____

_____

_____

_____

_____

Using the Internet, research the characteristics of one DHCP server software product:

1. Name of the product: _____

2. Manufacturer: _____

3. Retail price: _____

4. Summarize the product's purpose and functionality:

_____

_____

_____

_____

_____

Using the Internet, research the characteristics of one DNS server software product:

1. Name of the product: _____

2. Manufacturer: _____

3

3. Retail price: _____

4. Summarize the product's purpose and functionality:

_____

_____

_____

_____

_____

Using the Internet, research the characteristics of one proxy server software product:

1. Name of the product: _____

2. Manufacturer: _____

3. Retail price: _____

4. Summarize the product's purpose and functionality:

_____

_____

_____

_____

_____

Using the Internet, research the characteristics of one e-mail server software product:

1. Name of the product: _____

2. Manufacturer: _____

3. Retail price: _____

4. Summarize the product's purpose and functionality:

_____

_____

_____

_____

_____

Using the Internet, research the characteristics of one FTP server software product:

1. Name of the product: _____

2. Manufacturer: _____

3. Retail price: _____

4. Summarize the product's purpose and functionality:

_____

_____

_____

_____

_____

Using the Internet, research the characteristics of one list server software product:

1. Name of the product: _____

2. Manufacturer: _____

3. Retail price: _____

4. Summarize the product's purpose and functionality:

_____

_____

_____

_____

_____

Using the Internet, research the characteristics of one caching server software product:

1. Name of the product: _____

2. Manufacturer: _____

3. Retail price: _____

4. Summarize the product's purpose and functionality:

_____

_____

_____

_____

_____

Using the Internet, research the characteristics of one newsgroup server software product:

1. Name of the product: _____

2. Manufacturer: _____

3. Retail price: _____

4. Summarize the product's purpose and functionality:

_____

_____

_____

_____

_____

Using the Internet, research the characteristics of one web server software product:

1. Name of the product: _____

2. Manufacturer: _____

3. Retail price: _____

3

4. Summarize the product's purpose and functionality:

_____

_____

_____

_____

_____

Using the Internet, research the characteristics of one media server software product:

1. Name of the product: _____

2. Manufacturer: _____

3. Retail price: _____

4. Summarize the product's purpose and functionality:

_____

_____

_____

_____

_____

Using the Internet, research the characteristics of one LDAP server software product:

1. Name of the product: _____

2. Manufacturer: _____

3. Retail price: _____

4. Summarize the product's purpose and functionality:

_____

_____

_____

_____

_____

Certification Objectives:

Objectives for the i–Net+ exam:

➤ Understand and be able to describe the concept of caching and its implications.

➤ Identify problems with Internet connectivity from source to destination for various types of servers.

➤ Understand how various protocols or services apply to the function of their corresponding server, such as a mail server, a web server, or a file transfer server.

➤ Understand and be able to describe the capabilities of application server providers.

Review Questions

1. A DHCP server and a web server are required for an ISP to host customers' web pages. True or False?

2. A proxy server and a web server are two different names for the same type of server. True or False?

3. A certificate server and a list server are similar because they both must manage many e-mail addresses. True or False?

4. A DHCP server and a DNS server both have IP-address-related functions. True or False?

5. Which types of servers does an ISP need if they want to offer both news and e-mail services to their customers?

   _____

   _____

   _____

   _____

   _____

6. The owner of a small firm wants his firm's intranet to have the same name lookup service that is used on the Internet. What type of server does this company owner need?

   _____

   _____

   _____

   _____

   _____

LAB 3.5 INSTALLING THE APACHE WEB SERVER

Objectives

In its most simple form, a web server runs software that allows it to deliver documents and graphics that have been formatted using HTML or another compatible markup language to a client's web browser.

The Apache Web Server is free web server software created and maintained by the Apache Software Foundation. It can run on UNIX and Windows 98/NT/2000 computers.

After completing this lab, you will be able to:

➤ Install Apache Web Server

➤ Start Apache Web Server

➤ Stop Apache Web Server

➤ Test your Apache Web Server installation

3

Materials Required

This lab will require the following:

➤ Windows 2000

➤ A lab workgroup size of 2–4 students

➤ Microsoft Internet Explorer 5 or later

➤ Your lab workstation must be configured with an IP address on an intranet or the Internet.

 Due to the constantly changing environment of the Internet, exact download URLs cannot be provided for this lab. The Apache Web Server is a free download available at *http://apache.org*. See the web site for more details and download instructions.

Estimated completion time: **45 minutes**

ACTIVITY

Installing Apache Web Server:

1. Double-click the Apache Web Server executable to begin the installation.

2. Click **Next**.

3. Click **Yes** after reading the license agreement.

4. Click **Next**.

5. Click **Next**.

6. Click **Complete**, and then click **Next**.

7. Click **Install**.

8. Click **Finish**.

Starting Apache Web Server:

1. Click **Start**.

2. Point to **Programs**.

3. Point to **Apache httpd Server**, and then point to **Control Apache Server**.

4. Click **Start**.

Testing your Apache Web Server installation:

1. Double-click **Internet Explorer**.

2. In the Address box, type **http://###.##.##.##**, where the # signs represent your lab workstation's IP address, and then press **Enter**.

Stopping Apache Web Server:

1. Click **Start**.

2. Point to **Programs**.

3. Point to **Apache httpd Server**, and then point to **Control Apache Server**.

4. Click **Stop**.

Certification Objectives:

Objectives for the i–Net+ exam:

➤ Assist in the administration of Internet/intranet sites.

➤ Test pre-production Web and e-commerce servers.

Review Questions

1. Apache Web Server is cross-platform—meaning that it can be run using many different operating systems. True or False?

2. A web server provides HTML-formatted documents and graphics to client web browsers. True or False?

3. By starting the Apache Web Server software, you are instructing the web server to display web pages. True or False?

4. If you simply install Apache and start it, no web pages will be displayed. True or False?

5. If you are running a web site for a small business and stop the Apache server, no external e-mail will be delivered until you restart the Apache server. True or False?

6. What are the advantages and disadvantages of using free software for your web server needs?

_____

_____

_____

_____

_____

SIGHTS AND SOUNDS OF THE INTERNET

Labs included in this chapter

➤ Lab 4.1 Adding Sound to Your Web Site

➤ Lab 4.2 Image Mapping

➤ Lab 4.3 Adding a Movie to Your Web Site

---

i-Net+ Exam Objectives	
Objective	**Lab**
Create HTML pages.	4.1, 4.2, 4.3
Identify when to use various multimedia extensions or plug-ins.	4.1, 4.3
Identify when to use various image and multimedia file formats.	4.3

LAB 4.1 ADDING SOUND TO YOUR WEB SITE

Objectives

Adding sound to your web site will make it stand out from the competition. To create effective sound for your site, you must know the following:

➤ **MIDI (Musical Instrument Digital Interface):** A standard for transmitting sound from musical devices, such as electronic keyboards, to computers where it can be digitally stored.

➤ **MP3:** A high-quality audio/video format that uses MPEG, Version 3 technology to compress data.

➤ **WAV file:** A Windows audio file commonly used on web sites for short, low-quality sound.

➤ **RMF:** A proprietary audio file format developed by Beatnik. It requires a Beatnik Player plug-in on the client, and is supported by Netscape Navigator.

➤ **Sampling:** Part of the process of converting sound or video from analog to digital format, whereby a sound wave or image is measured at uniform time intervals and saved as a series of smaller representative blocks.

➤ **AIFF file:** A sound file that uses a format originally developed for Apple computers.

➤ **AU file:** A sound file that uses a format originally developed for UNIX computers.

After completing this lab, you will be able to:

➤ Add downloadable sound files to a web site

➤ Add background music to a web site

➤ Define common sound file terminology

Materials Required

This lab will require the following:

➤ Windows 9x, 2000, or Windows NT

➤ A lab workgroup size of 2–4 students

➤ One web server

➤ Each lab workstation must have a sound card and speakers installed

➤ One directory for each student on an intranet or Internet web server

➤ Microsoft Internet Explorer 5 or later installed on each lab computer

4

➤ Students must be able to map a network drive to their assigned share on the web server and be provided the UNC path to connect. Each student must also be provided the URL to view their personal web directory.

➤ The web server must be configured to use the name "index.html" and the index page for each student's personal web directory.

➤ Each lab computer must have one sound file on its desktop named "Websound.mid." Students will publish this graphic on the web server.

Estimated completion time: **45 minutes**

ACTIVITY

Adding background music to index.html:

1. Click **Start**, and then click **Run**.

2. Type **Notepad**, and then click **OK**.

3. Type **<HTML>**, and then press **Enter**.

4. Press **Enter** twice.

5. Type **<BGSOUND SRC="Websound.mid" LOOP="1" VOLUME="0">**, and then press **Enter**.

6. Press **Enter** twice, and then type **</HTML>**.

7. Click **File** on the menu bar, and then click **Save As**. Select the location where you want to save the file.

8. In the File Name: text box, type **index.html**.

9. Click **OK**.

10. Publish both index.html *and* Websound.mid to your personal web directory.

11. Open Internet Explorer by double-clicking its icon on your desktop.

12. Type the URL of your personal web directory, and then press **Enter**. After your web page has loaded you should be able to hear the background music you added. If you do not hear background music, check your HTML syntax by repeating Steps 1–10.

13. Close Internet Explorer.

Adding downloadable music to index.html:

If your browser has a plug-in installed, the multimedia file may play automatically.

1. Click **Start**, and then click **Run**.

2. Type **Notepad**, and then click **OK**.

3. Click **File** on the menu bar, and then click **Open**. Select the appropriate folder.

4. Click the **Files of Type** drop-down arrow, and then click **All Files**.

5. Double-click **index.html**.

6. Move the insertion point to a position in the index.html file where you want to add a hyperlink.

7. Type **<A HREF="Websound.mid">Backgroud Music</a>**, and then press **Enter**.

8. Save the change to index.html.

9. Publish both index.html *and* Websound.mid to your personal web directory.

10. Open Internet Explorer by double-clicking its icon on your desktop, type the URL to your personal web directory, and then test your new hyperlink.

11. Close Internet Explorer.

Certification Objectives:

Objectives for the i-Net+ exam:

➤ Create HTML pages.

➤ Identify when to use various multimedia extensions or plug-ins.

Review Questions

1. <BACKGROUND_SOUND="filename"> is the HTML tag used to apply background sound to a Web site for viewing using Internet Explorer. True or False?

2. A hyperlink tag can be used to publish sound files for download. True or False?

3. MIDI, WAV, and MP3 are each different types of formats that can be used to store sound. True or False?

4. Some versions of Netscape and Internet Explorer require different HTML tags to apply background sound to a web page. True or False?

5. The Rich Music Format is a proprietary audio file format. True or False?

6. In your own words, describe what the term "sampling" means.

_____

_____

_____

_____

_____

4

LAB 4.2 IMAGE MAPPING

Objectives

An image map is a graphic on a web page that contains one or more embedded hyper-links. The map tag is used when you identify the name and areas of a client-side image map. Each map tag contains one or more AREA (A) elements that identify the geometrical regions that work as hot spots or clickable areas which can link to other web documents. In addition to linking to another web document, the map tag can be used to execute scripts or commands when various events occur. Some of the attributes used to define these events include the following:

➤ Onclick=script name

➤ Ondblclick=script name

➤ Onkeydown=script name

➤ Onkeypress=script name

➤ Onkeyup=script name

➤ Onmousedown=script name

➤ Onmousemove=script name

➤ Onmouseout=script name

➤ Onmouseover=script name

➤ Onmouseup=script name

Note that GIF89a is a GIF image version that supports animation, transparent backgrounds, and interlacing. A GIF89a is more commonly called an animated gif.

After completing this lab, you will be able to:

➤ Create an image-mapped graphic.

➤ Link an image-mapped graphic to a script or web document.

➤ Define common image-mapping terms.

Materials Required

This lab will require the following:

➤ Windows 9x, 2000, or Windows NT

➤ A lab workgroup size of 2–4 students

➤ Microsoft FrontPage 2000

➤ Microsoft Internet Explorer 5 or later installed on each lab computer

➤ A shortcut to Microsoft FrontPage 2000 on the desktop of each computer

➤ A connection to the Internet for each computer

➤ Students must be able to map a network drive to their assigned share on the web server and be provided the UNC path to connect. Students must also be provided the URL to view their personal web directory. Each student's personal web share must also be a FrontPage 2000 Web.

➤ The web server must be configured to use the name "index.html" and the index page for each student's personal web directory.

Estimated completion time: **1 hour**

ACTIVITY

Connect to your FrontPage Web:

1. Double-click the **Microsoft FrontPage** icon found on your desktop.

2. Click **File** on the menu bar, and then click **Open Web**.

3. In the Folder name text box, type the web address to your personal FrontPage Web. Your instructor will provide the correct address to your personal web share. Click **Open**.

4. If you are prompted for a user name and password, type your logon information (provided by your instructor), and then click **OK**.

5. If you were required to enter a user name and password, click **OK** in the Open Web dialog box again. Your screen should display a folder list before continuing.

6. Click **File** on the menu bar, and then click **Open**.

7. Double-click **index.html**.

Adding a hyperlink to a graphic:

1. Click a graphic on the web page. Anchor points will appear. A toolbar will also appear at the bottom of the FrontPage window. This is the image map toolbar.

2. Click the **Rectangle Hotspot** on the image map toolbar. Your insertion point icon will change.

3. Click and hold down the mouse button on top of the graphic area that you want to hyperlink. Slowly move your mouse to create a rectangular shape on the graphic.

4. In the URL text box, type **http:www.microsoft.com**, and then press **Enter**.

5. Click **File** on the menu bar, and then click **Save**.

6. Publish **index.html** to your personal web directory. See your instructor for more details on this step.

4

7. Open Internet Explorer by double-clicking its icon on your desktop, and then type the URL to your personal web directory.

8. On the lines provided, describe the results.

_____

_____

_____

_____

_____

9. Close Internet Explorer.

Understanding image map tags:

1. Click **Start**, and then click **Run**.

2. Type **notepad**, and then click **OK**.

3. Click **File** on the menu bar, and then click **Open**.

4. Navigate to and double-click **index.html**.

5. On the lines provided, write the HTML code used to create an image map.

_____

_____

_____

_____

_____

_____

_____

_____

_____

_____

Certification Objectives:

Objectives for the i-Net+ exam:

➤ Create HTML pages.

Review Questions

1. Microsoft FrontPage 2000 has built-in tools that make it easier to create image-mapped graphics. True or False?

2. The map tag requires both a start and end tag. True or False?

3. The map tag utilizes coordinates to define a hot spot area. True or False?

4. Onmouseover is a attribute of the map tag, and can be used to initiate an action. True or False?

5. On the lines provided, write the code to image map a graphic named header.gif. The graphic must have two separate hot spots, each executing a script named logdb.pl. Use the following two events in your code to execute the script: Onclick=script name and Ondblclick=script name.

_____

_____

_____

_____

_____

_____

_____

_____

_____

6. What is the difference between an animated gif and an imaged-mapped gif?

_____

_____

_____

_____

_____

_____

_____

_____

Lab 4.3 Adding a Movie to Your Web Site

Objectives

To effectively add movies to your web sites, you need to know the following facts:

➤ An AVI (Audio Video Interleaved) file is an older Windows video format that is not as well compressed as more recent file formats such as MPEG or QuickTime.

➤ QuickTime is a popular video file format developed by Apple. QuickTime files have a .MOV file extension.

➤ Shockwave is a popular multimedia file format developed by Macromedia that produces video and audio streaming data.

➤ Streaming data is multimedia data that is played as it is being downloaded. Video conferencing and listening to the radio from the Web are two examples of streaming data.

4

➤ Real Time Streaming Protocol (RTSP) is a protocol that establishes and controls time-synchronized streams of continuous media such as audio and video. RTSP uses the RTP protocol and acts as a network remote control for multimedia servers.

➤ VRML (Virtual Reality Modeling Language) is a language used to create interactive animation on web sites. VRML is not as common as it once was, because it's easier for developers to use Flash or Shockwave plug-in software rather than developing their own code.

After completing this lab, you will be able to:

➤ Embed movie files into a web document

➤ Define common movie file terminology

Materials Required

Your lab will require the following:

➤ Windows 9x, 2000, or Windows NT

➤ A lab workgroup size of 2–4 students

➤ One web server

➤ One directory for each student on an intranet or Internet web server

➤ Microsoft Internet Explorer 5 or later installed on each lab computer

➤ Students must be able to map a network drive to their assigned share on the web server, and be provided the UNC path to connect. Students must also be provided the URL to view their personal web directory.

➤ The web server must be configured to use the name "index.html" and the index page for each student's personal web directory.

➤ Each lab computer must have one AVI file on their desktop named "Webmovie.avi." Students will publish this on the web server.

Estimated completion time: **45 minutes**

ACTIVITY

Embedding an AVI into index.html:

1. Click **Start**, and then click **Run**.

2. Type **Notepad**, and then click **OK**.

3. Click **File** on the menu bar, and then click **Open**.

4. Click the **Files of Type** drop-down arrow, and click **All Files**.

5. Double-click **index.html**.

6. Move the insertion point to a position in the index.html file where you want to add a hyperlink.

7. Type **< IMG BORDER="0" DYNSRC="Webmovie.avi" START="mouseover" WIDTH="478" HEIGHT="843" >**, and then press **Enter**.

8. Save the change to index.html.

9. Publish both **index.html** and **Webmovie.avi** to your personal web directory.

10. Open Internet Explorer by double-clicking its icon on your desktop, and then type the URL to your personal web directory.

11. On the line provided, describe the results.

   _____

12. Close Internet Explorer.

13. Using the information that you have learned, resize the windows of the embedded AVI by changing the width and height elements. Also, make the AVI begin when the web page is initially loaded by changing "mouseover" to **fileopen**.

Adding a downloadable AVI to index.html:

1. Click **Start**, and then click **Run**.

2. Type **Notepad**, and then click **OK**.

3. Click **File** on the menu bar, and then click **Open**.

4. Click the **Files of Type** drop-down arrow, and then click **All Files**.

5. Double-click **index.html**.

6. Move the insertion point to a position in the index.html file where you want to add a hyperlink.

7. Type **<A HREF="Webmovie.avi">Web movie </A>**, and then press **Enter**.

8. Save the changes to index.html.

9. Publish both **index.html** and **Webmovie.avi** to your personal web directory.

10. Open Internet Explorer by double-clicking its icon on your desktop, and then type the URL to your personal web directory.

11. On the line provided, describe the results.

   _____

12. Close Internet Explorer.

Certification Objectives:

Objectives for the i–Net+ exam:

➤ Create HTML pages.

➤ Identify when to use various multimedia extensions or plug-ins.

➤ Identify when to use various image and multimedia file formats.

Review Questions

1. The <A HREF> tag can be used to embed video files into a web document. True or False?

2. QuickTime was developed by Apple computers. True or False?

3. Shockwave, developed by Microsoft, is a popular multimedia file format that can produce streaming video and audio data. True or False?

4. The Real Time Streaming Protocol establishes and controls time-synchronized streams of continuous media, such as audio and video. True or False?

5. A developer can create interactive animation for a web site using VRML. True or False?

6. List five Macromedia software products that could be used to enhance a web site. (*Hint:* You can visit *www.macromedia.com.*)

   _____

   _____

   _____

   _____

   _____

WebTV and Other Internet Appliances

Labs included in this chapter
➤ Lab 5.1 Internet Appliances and Compatible Devices
➤ Lab 5.2 Understanding WAP and Writing a WAP-Compliant Web Page

i-Net+ Exam Objectives	
Objective	**Lab**
Use/configure Web browsers and other Internet/intranet clients, and be able to describe their use to others.	5.1
Create HTML pages	5.2
Identify the common formats used to deliver content to wireless devices.	5.2

71

LAB 5.1 INTERNET APPLIANCES AND COMPATIBLE DEVICES

Objectives

The goal of this lab activity is to familiarize you with some of the alternative methods available to access the Internet. Examples of Internet-compatible devices include PDA's, Internet-ready cellular phones, and Internet-ready pagers.

To understand this technology, you should know the following key items:

➤ **Internet appliance**: A device other than a computer that is used to access the Internet as a client with limited applications.

➤ **Internet-compatible device**: A device other than a computer that can be used to access the Internet but has other functionality. Examples include a cellular phone with Internet capability and a PDA with a wireless modem.

➤ **Interactive television**: A technology to combine a web browser such as WebTV with a television show so that a user can interact with a web site that is synchronized with a TV show.

➤ **WebTV**: A system for displaying information from the Internet on a television screen and to support interactive television.

➤ **WebTV for Windows**: A Windows component that supports television on a PC by way of a TV tuner card.

➤ **IP Telephony terminal**: A device such as a PC that can be used to initiate or receive voice communications over the Internet.

➤ **Public Switched Telephone Network (PSTN)**: The traditional public telephone network, which uses a circuit-switching technology.

After completing this lab exercise, you will be able to:

➤ Discuss the advantages and disadvantages of Internet appliances

➤ Describe interactive television and its limitations

➤ Identify and compare Internet-compatible devices to other Internet access methods

Materials Required

This lab will require the following:

➤ A pen and paper

Estimated completion time: **45 minutes**

ACTIVITY

Research an Internet appliance and find out the following information:

1. Name of the Internet appliance. _____

2. Manufacturer. _____

3. Retail price. _____

4. Briefly summarize all the capabilities of the Internet appliance.

   _____

   _____

   _____

   _____

   _____

Research a second Internet appliance and find out the following information:

1. Name of the Internet appliance. _____

2. Manufacturer. _____

3. Retail price. _____

4. Briefly summarize all the capabilities of the Internet appliance.

   _____

   _____

   _____

   _____

   _____

Choose one interactive television product and answer the following questions about it:

1. Name of the product. _____

2. Manufacturer. _____

3. Retail price. _____

4. Briefly summarize all the capabilities of the product.

   _____

   _____

   _____

   _____

   _____

Choose two Internet-compatible devices and answer the following questions about them:

1. Name of the first product. _____

2. Manufacturer. _____

3. Retail price. _____

4. Briefly summarize all of the capabilities of the product.

_____

_____

_____

_____

_____

1. Name of the second product. _____

2. Manufacturer. _____

3. Retail price. _____

4. Briefly summarize all of the capabilities of the product.

_____

_____

_____

_____

_____

Certification Objectives:

Objectives for the i-Net+ exam:

➤ Use/configure Web browsers and other Internet/intranet clients, and be able to describe their use to others.

Review Questions

1. All Internet appliances are compatible with interactive television. True or False?

2. A cellular phone that can connect to the Internet is an example of an Internet-compatible device. True or False?

3. Based on your research from the previous activity, which solution would you recommend for someone who only wanted to send and receive e-mail messages and had a limited budget. Explain your answer.

_____

_____

_____

_____

_____

4. On the lines provided, describe the difference between WebTV and WebTV for Windows.

_____

_____

_____

_____

_____

5. WebTV supports _____ television.

.5

LAB 5.2 UNDERSTANDING WAP AND WRITING A WAP-COMPLIANT WEB PAGE

Objectives

The goal of this lab is to provide you with the hands-on web development experience required to design and implement a web site for wireless WAP-compliant devices. Specifically, you will work with a phone simulator.

The Wireless Application protocol (WAP) is a protocol that specifies how information from the Internet is formatted, transmitted, and received by wireless Internet appliances. WML (Wireless Markup Language) is a markup language that is used to build web pages for transmission to wireless devices using the WAP protocol.

A card, as it applies to WML, is a section of a WML file (a deck) that fits on the screen of a wireless Internet device. A deck is a file containing text to be displayed on wireless Internet devices. A gateway is complex server that converts data from WML format to binary before the data is transmitted to a wireless devices. Figure 5-1 illustrates how a gateway acts as an intermediary between the Internet and wireless devices.

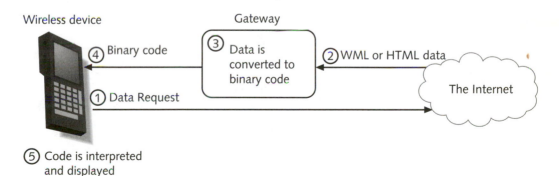

Figure 5-1   How wireless devices use the WAP specifications to access the Internet

After completing this lab, you will be able to:

➤ Describe the relationship between WML and WAP

➤ Install a phone simulator for Windows

➤ Create and publish a WML web page

➤ Use a phone simulator for Windows to WML web pages

Materials Required

This lab will require the following:

➤ Windows 9x

➤ A lab workgroup size of 2–4 students

➤ One directory for each student on an intranet or Internet web server

➤ Microsoft Internet Explorer 5 or later installed on each lab computer

➤ Students must be able to map a network drive to their assigned share on the web server, and be provided the UNC path to connect. Students must also be provided the URL to view their personal web directory in a browser window.

➤ Students must understand how to publish a web document to their personal web share, or the instructor must provide additional instructions.

➤ Due to the constantly changing environment of the Internet, exact download URLs weren't provided for this lab. The phone simulator you need is a free download available at *http://developer.openwave.com*. See the web site for more details and download instructions.

➤ The MIME types in Table 5-1 must be configured on the student web server before WML web pages will be displayed correctly using the phone simulator. Refer to your web server documentation for more information about configuring MIME types.

Table 5-1   MIME types

Content	MIME Type	File Extension
WML	text/vnd.wap.wml	.wml
WML script	text/vnd.wap.wmlscript	.wmls
BMP image	image/bmp	.bmp
WBMP image	image/vnd.wap.wbmp	.wbmp

Estimated completion time: **45 minutes**

ACTIVITY
Install the phone simulator for Windows:

Before installing the phone simulator, you must first download the installation files. The following installation instructions were created using UP.SDK 4.1. If you are installing a different version, the exact steps may vary slightly.

1. Double-click the **UP.Browser** executable file.

2. Click **Next**.

3. Click **Yes**.

4. Click **Yes**.

5. Check the **Yes** check box, and then click **Next**.

6. Click **Next**.

7. Click **Next**.

8. Click **Finish**.

Creating a WML web page:

1. Click **Start**, and then click **Run**.

2. Type **Notepad**, and then click **OK**.

3. Type **<?xml version= "1.0"?>**, and then press **Enter**.

4. Type **<!DOCTYPE wml PUBLIC "-//PHONE.COM//DTD WML 1.1//EN"**, and then press **Enter**.

5. Type **http://www.phone.com/dtd/wml11.dtd >**, and then press **Enter**.

6. Type **<wml>**, and then press **Enter**.

7. Type **<card>**, and then press **Enter**.

8. Type **<p>Hello <i> Wireless</i> World!</p>**, and then press **Enter**.

9. Type **<do type="accept" label="Next">**, and then press **Enter**.

10. Type **<go href="#c2"/>**, and then press **Enter**.

11. Type **</do>**, and then press **Enter**.

12. Type **</card>**, and then press **Enter**.

13. Type **<card id="c2">**, and then press **Enter**.

14. Type **<p> This is CARD 2 </p>**, and then press **Enter**.

15. Type **</card>**, and then press **Enter**.

16. Type **</wml>**, and then press **Enter**. Your wml code should now match the example shown in Figure 5-2.

```
<?xml version="1.0"?>
<!DOCTYPE wml PUBLIC "-//PHONE.COM//DTD WML 1.1//EN"
                 "http://www.phone.com/dtd/wml11.dtd">

<wml>
<card>
<p>Hello<i>Wireless</i>World!</p>
<do type="accept" label="Next">
<go href="#c2"/>
</do>

</card>
<card id="c2">
<p>This is CARD 2</p>
</card>
</wml>
```

Figure 5-2   Sample Index.wml

17. Click **File** on the menu bar, and then click **Save As**. Click the **Save in:** drop-down arrow, and then click **Desktop**.

18. Click the **Save as type:** drop-down arrow, and then click **All Files**.

19. Type **index.wml** in the File Name: text box, and then click **Save**.

20. Publish index.wml to your personal web directory.

Test your web page:

1. Click **Start**, point to **Programs**, point to **UP.SDK 4.1**, and then click **UP.Simulator**. Your program group (UP.SDK 4.1) may be named differently depending on the version of software you installed.

2. In the Go! text box, type **http://*yoururl*/index.wml** (where *yoururl* is your URL), and then press **Enter**.

3. Describe the results on the lines provided.

_____

_____

Certification Objectives:

Objectives for the i-Net+ exam:

➤ Create HTML pages.

➤ Identify the common formats used to deliver content to wireless devices.

Review Questions

1. WAP is a markup language used to build web pages for transmission to wireless devices. True or False?

2. A WML file can contain multiple cards. True or False?

3. A card is equal to one screen on a wireless device. True or False?

4. A gateway converts data from one format to another. True or False?

5. On the lines provided, write the WML code to add a third card containing the words "THIRD CARD" to the WML page you created during the previous activity.

_____

_____

_____

_____

_____

6. In the previous activity, what effect did the <i>Wireless</i> tag have on the word "Wireless"?

_____

_____

_____

_____

_____

5

6 UNDERSTANDING NETWORKS

Labs included in this chapter

➤ Lab 6.1 Networking Components

➤ Lab 6.2 Understanding Topologies

➤ Lab 6.3 Virtual Communication and the OSI Model

---

i-Net+ Exam Objectives	
Objective	**Lab**
Understand and be able to describe the core components of the Internet infrastructure.	6.1, 6.3
Identify when to use various diagnostic tools for resolving Internet problems.	6.1
Create a logic diagram of Internet components from the client to the server.	6.1
Describe the various hardware and software connection devices and when to use them.	6.1
Understand and be able to describe how common networking topologies are used.	6.2

LAB 6.1 NETWORKING COMPONENTS

Objectives

During this lab you will familiarize yourself with many common components, such as cable, of a networked environment. To effectively work with cable, you should know the following:

> ➤ A packet is a segment of network data that includes a header, destination address, and trailer information. Packets are sent as a unit using electronic communication over wire or fiber-optic cables.

> ➤ Unshielded twisted-pair (UTP) is a cable that is made of one or more twisted pairs of wires and that is not surrounded by a metal shield.

> ➤ Shielded twisted-pair (STP) is a cable that is made of one or more twisted pairs of wires and that is surrounded by a metal shield.

> ➤ 100BaseT is an Ethernet standard that operates at 100 Mbps and uses STP cabling. It's also called Fast Ethernet.

> ➤ 100BaseFX is a variation of 100BaseT that supports fiber-optic cable.

> ➤ 10Base2 is an Ethernet standard that operates at 10 Mbps and uses small coaxial cable up to 200 meters long. It's also called Thinnet.

> ➤ 10Base5 is an Ethernet standard that operates at 10 Mbps and uses thick coaxial cable up to 500 meters long. It's also called Thicknet.

> ➤ RJ is an acronym for registered jack. An RJ connector is used to connect cables such as telephone wire (RJ11) and UTP wire (RJ45). The number that appears after the letters "RJ" identifies the size of the RJ connecter.

In addition to the nuances of cabling, you should know the following:

> ➤ A hub is a network device used to join nodes of a LAN together. There are three types of hubs: passive hubs, active hubs, and intelligent hubs.

> ➤ A gateway is a device that allows two networks of different protocols to communicate. A gateway can translate a protocol by reading a packet and encapsulating its data into a new packet, which can be understood by the destination network.

> ➤ While a hub simply interconnects nodes at a single site, a bridge is used to interconnect nodes at different sites. It is important to understand that a bridge will never translate packet data.

> ➤ A router can perform the same functions as a bridge, and more. When a router receives a packet of data, it not only determines the appropriate network, but also identifies the best available route for the packet to travel.

> ➤ A brouter is a hybrid networking device, which combines the functionality of both a router and bridge.

➤ A switch is a network device that can identify the next destination of a packet and forward the packet to that destination. The difference between a switch and a router is that a router will examine the entire route of a packet, whereas a switch will examine only the next immediate destination.

➤ A hop is any trip that a packet makes between two network devices.

➤ A repeater is a network device that receives an electromagnetic signal, amplifies the signal, and then retransmits the signal.

➤ In the networking environment, bandwidth refers to the amount of data that can be sent or received over a given type of transmission medium at any given time. Bandwidth is usually expressed in bits per second (bps), kilobits per second (Kbps), or megabits per second (Mbps). Table 6-1 describes some common technologies and their bandwidth.

6

Table 6-1   Common bandwidth technologies

Technology	Maximum Throughput Speeds	Common Uses
GSM mobile telephone service	9.6 to 14.4 Kbps	Wireless technology used for personal and business mobile telephones
Regular telephone (POTS)	Up to 56 Kbps	Home and small business access to an ISP using a modem
X.25	56 Kbps	Provides communication between mainframes and terminals
ISDN	64 Kbps to 128 Kbps	Small- to medium-sized business access to an ISP
IDSL	128 Kbps	(ISDN Digital Subscriber Line) Home and small business access to an ISP
DSL Lite or G.Lite	Up to 384 Kbps upstream and up to 6 Mbps downstream	Less-expensive version of DSL
ADSL	640 Kbps upstream and up to 6.1 Mbps downstream	(Asymmetric Digital Subscriber Line) Most bandwidth is from ISP to user
SDSL	1.544 Mbps	(Symmetric DSL) Equal bandwidths in both directions
HDSL	Up to 3 Mbps	(High bit-rate DSL) Equal bandwidths in both directions
Cable modem	512 Kbps to 5 Mbps	Home or small business to ISP
VDSL	Up to 55 Mbps over short distances	(Very high data rate DSL) Future technology of DSL under development
Frame Relay	56 Kbps to 45 Mbps	Businesses that need to communicate internationally or across the country

Table 6-1   Common bandwidth technologies (continued)

Technology	Maximum Throughput Speeds	Common Uses
Fractional T1	N times 64 Kbps (where n = number of channels or portions of a T1 leased)	Companies expecting to grow into a T1 line, but not yet ready for a T1
T1	1.544 Mbps	To connect large companies to branch offices or an ISP
Token Ring	4 or 16 Mbps	Used for local network
Ethernet	10 or 100 Mbps	Most popular technology for a local network
T3	45 Mbps	Large companies that require a lot of bandwidth and transmit extensive amounts of data
OC-1	52 Mbps	ISP to regional ISP
FDDI	100 Mbps	Supports network backbones from the 1980s and early 1990s. Also used to connect LANs across multiple buildings
ATM	25, 45, 155, or 622 Mbps	Large business WANs and LAN backbones
OC-3	155 Mbps	Internet or large corporation backbone
Gigabit Ethernet	1 Gbps	New under-development technology
OC-24	1.23 Gbps	Internet backbone uses optical fiber
OC-256	13 Gbps	Major Internet backbone uses optical fiber
SONET	51, 155, 622, 1244, or 2480 Mbps	(Synchronous Optical Network) Major backbones

After completing this lab, you will be able to:

➤ Identify common networking components

➤ Describe the function of common networking components

➤ Draw a logical diagram depicting the travel of a packet through a network

Materials Required

This lab will require the following:

➤ Your instructor will provide five of the following items for demonstration purposes during this lab activity:

- RJ-11
- RJ-45
- One hub
- One repeater
- One router

- One switch
- One bridge
- One brouter
- Network analyzer
- Fiber-optic cable and connectors
- Any type of ISDN device
- Any type of DSL device
- Thicknet cable
- Unshielded twisted-pair wire
- Shielded twisted-pair wire

6

Estimated completion time: **45 minutes**

ACTIVITY

Identify network components:

1. Examine the five demonstration devices provided by your instructor. Describe the function of each device and explain how each could be used in a networked environment:

Item 1

_____

_____

_____

Item 2

_____

_____

_____

Item 3

_____

_____

_____

Item 4

_____

_____

_____

Item 5

_____

_____

_____

_____

Draw a logic diagram from client to sever:

1. In the space provided, draw a diagram depicting the route of a packet traveling through a network. Beginning from a home DSL connection, the packet must travel through two routers, a repeater, and a bridge in order to connect to a web server. Be sure to include each of these network devices in your diagram.

Certification Objectives:

Objectives for the i-Net+ Exam:

> ➤ Understand and be able to describe the core components of the Internet infrastructure.

> ➤ Identify when to use various diagnostic tools for resolving Internet problems.

> ➤ Create a logic diagram of Internet components from the client to the server.

> ➤ Describe the various hardware and software connection devices and when to use them.

Review Questions

1. A hub is a networking device that passes all incoming packets to all outbound ports. True or False?

2. RJ is an acronym for registered jack. True or False?

3. RJ-45 connectors are often used in a LAN environment. True or False?

4. A bridge translates packets to join two networks. True or False?

5. A packet is a data segment used to communicate on a network. True or False?

6. Describe the difference between UTP and STP.

   _____

   _____

   _____

   _____

   _____

7. Describe the difference between a router and a hub.

   _____

   _____

   _____

   _____

   _____

LAB 6.2 UNDERSTANDING TOPOLOGIES

Objectives

The objective of this lab is to familiarize you with these primary network topologies: bus, star, ring, and mesh. As you become more familiar with topologies, you'll need the following information:

➤ The term "LAN" is an acronym for local area network. LAN normally refers to a small or medium-sized network that is contained within a small geographical area. Most modern LAN's use Category 5 UTP with RJ-45 connectors.

➤ The term "WAN" is an acronym for wide area network. WAN normally refers to a network that is spread across a large geographical area.

➤ The term "MAN" stands for metropolitan area network. MAN is normally used to refer to a small or medium-sized network that is contained within a metropolitan area.

You should also know that the most simple network topology is the bus network. To communicate on a bus network, a node broadcasts a packet that tells to whom the message is being sent. All other nodes on the bus can "read" the frame. When a node "reads" a frame addressed to itself, it copies the frame off the bus. A terminator is required at the end of a bus network, as shown in Figure 6-1.

Terminator   Terminator

Figure 6-1   Bus topology

Unlike the bus topology, the star topology connects all network nodes to a single hub. Figure 6-2 shows four computers connected to a single hub. Network nodes communicate by sending packets to a hub, which then disperses them to all outing ports.

Figure 6-2   Star topology

The ring, a less-popular topology, connects network nodes in a single circle. Network devices, such as MSAUs (multistation access units), are used to connect the two ends of a ring network. Figure 6-3 shows how an MSAU is implemented on a ring network. Because communication is from node-to-node in one direction around a Token Ring network, any single network node failure can have an impact on the entire network.

Of all these topologies, the most redundant and reliable topology is the mesh topology. A mesh topology connects each node to every other node using separate cabling. This complex configuration provides redundant network paths in such a way that if one network segment fails, data can simply be rerouted.

After completing this lab, you will be able to:

➤ Describe the bus topology

➤ Describe the star topology

➤ Describe the ring topology

➤ Describe the mesh topology

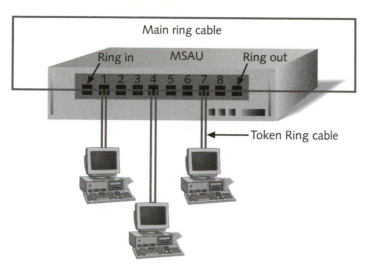

Figure 6-3   A Token Ring topology

Materials Required

This lab will require the following:

➤ Paper and pencil

Estimated completion time: **30 minutes**

ACTIVITY

1. Using what you have learned, draw a bus network that has five computers and five printers on the network. Don't forget to include a terminator.

2. Using what you have learned, draw a star network that has an eight-port hub, five computers, and two printers.

3. Using what you have learned, draw a ring network that has one MSAU, three computers, and one printer.

4. Using what you have learned, draw a ring network that has 10 computers.

Certification Objectives:

Objectives for the i-Net+ exam:

➤ Understand and be able to describe how common networking topologies are used.

Review Questions

1. A node failure in a token network can impact the entire network. True or False?

2. Star, ring, and bus network topologies require a terminator to prevent signal bounce. True or False?

3. MAU's are used to connect network nodes on ring networks. True or False?

4. Two office buildings across the street from each other that share an intranet could be on a MAN. True or False?

5. The Internet is one large-scale example of the Token Ring network topology. True or False?

6. A star network requires at least one hub. True or False?

Lab 6.3 Virtual Communication and the OSI Model

Objectives

After completing this lab, you will be able to define virtual communication and describe the function of each layer in the OSI model. Each layer of the OSI model is modularly independent, which means that processing at each layer is unaware of the other processes that may occur before or after it has completed its function. This behavior creates virtual communication between the source and destination computers for each layer of the OSI model.

The OSI model is composed of seven layers:

➤ **Application**: This layer of the OSI model is responsible for interfacing with application software such as web browsers or web servers.

➤ **Presentation**: This layer receives requests for files from the Application layer and presents the requests to the Session layer. The Presentation layer reformats, compresses, or encrypts data as necessary.

➤ **Session**: This layer is responsible for establishing and maintaining a session between two networked stations or hosts. A session between two hosts on a network is called a socket. When a session is established, a socket is opened. A disconnected session is called a closed socket.

➤ **Transport**: This layer is responsible for error checking and requests retransmission of data if it detects errors. The Transport layer is controlled by TCP (Transmission Control Protocol) and, to a lesser degree, by UDP (User Datagram Protocol).

➤ **Network**: This layer is responsible for dividing a block of data into segments that are small enough to travel over a network. These segments of data are called data packets, or datagrams. They contain data and special identifying information in headers and trailers at the beginning and end of the packet.

➤ **Data Link**: This layer is responsible for receiving packets of data from the Network layer and presenting them to the Physical layer for transport. If the packets are too large for the Physical layer, the Data Link layer splits them up into even smaller packets than did the Network layer. On the receiving end, the Data Link layer reconstructs the packets into their original size.

➤ **Physical**: This layer is responsible for passing data packets onto the cabling media. At this level, data is nothing but indistinguishable bits.

Note that virtual communication is the logical connection between two different locations. For example, in Figure 6-4, there is a logical connection, or virtual communication, between the post office mail box (input location) and the post office box (output location).

Notice the direction of the dotted arrow in Figure 6-5. As data travels from the PC to the server, it must traverse all seven layers of the OSI model so that it can be properly coded and sequenced to travel across the Internet. At each layer, specific processing occurs before the data is sent to the next layer. When the server receives the data, the data must again traverse all seven layers of the OSI model to be properly decoded and interpreted back into its original form.

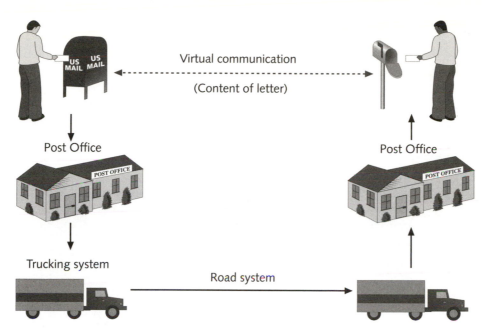

Figure 6-4 Communication is virtual between sender and receiver, but direct between adjacent system in the Postal Service

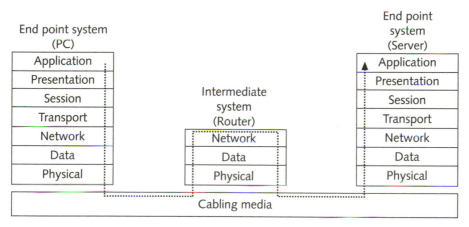

Figure 6-5 As data travels across the Internet, it traverses all seven OSI layers

After completing this lab, you will be able to:

➤ Define virtual communication as it applies to the OSI model

➤ Define and describe each layer of the OSI model

Materials Required

This lab will require the following:

➤ Pen or pencil

Estimated completion time: **45 minutes**

ACTIVITY

1. In the space provided, draw a diagram depicting virtual communication between two people using the Internet to send e-mail messages. In your diagram, the input and output device should be a computer, and the Internet should be represented using a cloud shape.

2. Complete the diagram in Figure 6-6. Title each box with the name of the layer and, in your own words, write a brief description of the processing that occurs at that layer. Your descriptions should be placed above the dotted lines.

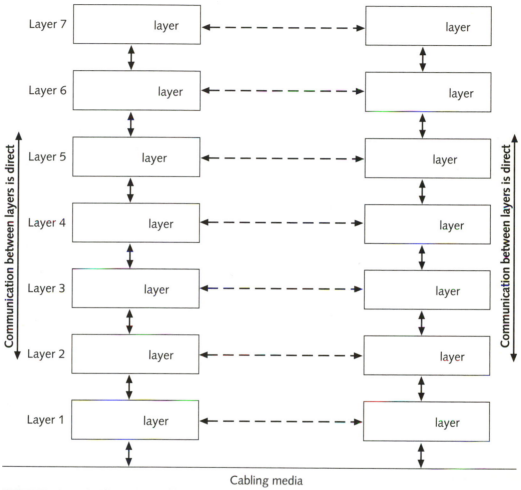

Figure 6-6   Processing diagram

Certification Objectives:

Objectives for the i-Net+ Exam:

> ➤ Understand and be able to describe the core components of the Internet infra-
> structure.

Review Questions

1. When a packet is encoded for travel across a network or the Internet, the packet traverses all seven layers of the OSI model, beginning with the Application layer. True or False?

2. At each layer of the OSI model, a data packet is completely decoded and then encoded again. True or False?

3. At times the Data Link layer will break packets into smaller bits for transmission by the Physical layer. True or False?

4. The Transport layer is responsible for error checking, retransmission of data, and guaranteeing successful data delivery. True or False?

5. TCP/IP and all other network protocols utilize all seven layers of the OSI model. True or False?

6. In your own words, describe the term virtual communication.

_____
_____
_____
_____
_____

INTERNET INFRASTRUCTURE

Labs included in this chapter

➤ Lab 7.1 Understanding IP Addressing

➤ Lab 7.2 Documenting an IP Network

➤ Lab 7.3 Understanding the Domain Name Service (DNS)

i-Net+ Exam Objectives	
Objective	**Lab**
Understand and be able to describe the infrastructure needed to support an Internet client.	7.1, 7.3
Understand and be able to describe the core components of the Internet infrastructure.	7.1, 7.2
Identify when to use various diagnostic tools for resolving Internet problems.	7.2, 7.3
Describe various hardware and software connection devices and when to use them.	7.2
Understand and be able to describe the use of Internet domain names and DNS.	7.3

LAB 7.1 UNDERSTANDING IP ADDRESSING

Objectives

The objective of this lab is to learn how to convert decimal numbers to and from binary format. It is important to understand how to convert decimal numbers to binary because IP addresses are binary addresses stored in decimal format. In addition to understanding IP addresses and learning how to convert them, you will also learn how to determine the class, or range, of an IP address.

IP addresses are 32-bit binary addresses that have been converted to decimal format so that they are easier for humans to understand. Binary may seem overwhelming at first, but you will soon see that it is simply a base-2 numbering system that can be easily converted to decimal.

Prior to beginning this lab, you must know the following:

➤ MAC (Media Access Control) is an element of the Data Link layer protocol that provides compatibility with the NIC used by the Physical layer. A network card address is often called a MAC address.

➤ A MAC address is a 6-byte hex hardware address unique to each NIC card and assigned by manufacturers. The address is often printed on the adapter. An example is 00 00 0C 08 2F 35. A MAC address is sometimes also called a physical address or hardware address.

➤ An IP address is a 32-bit address consisting of four numbers separated by periods and is used to uniquely identify a device on a network that uses TCP/IP protocols. The first numbers identify the network; the last numbers identify a host.

➤ An octet is an 8-bit number that is part of an IP address. IP addresses are composed of four 8-bit numbers, separated by periods.

➤ A protocol is a set of rules for communication used by a computer program. Some common forms of communication, or protocols, used on the Internet include the Hypertext Transfer Protocol (HTTP), File Transfer Protocol (FTP), and Telnet and Internet Relay Chat (IRC).

➤ DNS (Domain Name Service) is a distributed pool of information (called the name space) that keeps track of assigned domain names and their corresponding IP addresses. It is the system that allows a host to locate information in the pool.

In addition, you must know that IP addresses are used to uniquely identify TCP/IP hosts on a network. Your lab computer is an example of a TCP/IP host.

Before you learn the details of binary, you must understand what an IP address looks like and how it is formed. All IP addresses are 32-bits long, made up of four 8-bit numbers separated by periods. The largest possible 8-bit number is 11111111, which is equal to 255 in decimal, so the largest possible IP address in decimal format is 255.255.255.255. There are several reserved numbers in the range of all possible IP addresses. 255.255.255.225 and 127.0.0.1 are two examples.

In an IP address, each of the four numbers separated by periods is called an octet (for 8 bits), and each can be any number from 0 to 255, making for a total of 4.3 billion potential IP addresses. Beginning to feel a little lost? Well, not everyone is a mathematician, so let's try a short and easy way of reading binary and converting it to decimal format.

First, let's try converting this binary number to decimal format: 00110000. Does it look like garble? No problem. Binary is a base-2 number system that uses a combination of two digits, 0 and 1, to express values. Therefore, in binary, 1 isn't necessarily equal to the decimal value of 1. Think of it more as an on/off switch. If the bit (digit) is 1, then that number position is turned on, and its exponential value should be included when calculating its decimal equivalent. Otherwise, the value is 0 and turned off, meaning that it is just a placeholder and should be ignored.

In Table 7-1, the binary number 00110000 contains six bits that are off (ignored) and two bits that are on (equal to 1). To arrive at the decimal value of 00110000, we ignore the bits turned off (equal to zero) and exponentially increase the bits that are turned on, adding the results. We can easily use the information in Table 7-1 to determine the decimal equivalent of any bit in an octet.

7

Table 7-1   The exponential values of an octet

Binary value	Power of 2	Decimal value
00000001	2^0	1
00000010	2^1	2
00000100	2^2	4
00001000	2^3	8
00010000	2^4	16
00100000	2^5	32
01000000	2^6	64
10000000	2^7	128

In Table 7-2, we add the decimal result of 2^5 (32) and the decimal result of 2^4 (16) to get a total of 48, which is the correct decimal representation of the binary number 00110000.

Table 7-2   Converting 00110000 from binary to decimal

	Binary number	128	64	32	16	8	4	2	1	Decimal
Example	00110000	0	0	1	1	0	0	0	0	32 + 16 = 48

An IP address class is a range of addresses used to assign IP addresses to organizations. In addition to the three classes shown in Table 7-3, there are two more classes that aren't available for general use.

Table 7-3   Classes of IP addresses

Class	Network Octets (blanks in the IP address are used for octets identifying hosts)	Total Number of Possible Networks or Licenses	Host Octets (blanks in the IP address are used for octets identifying networks)	Total Number of Possible IP Addresses in Each Network
A	0.___.___.___ to 126.___.___.___	127	___.0.0.1 to ___.255.255.254	16 million
B	128.0.___.___ to 191.255.___.___	16,000	___.___.0.1 to ___.___.255.254	65,000
C	192.0.0.___ to 223.255.255.___	2,000,000	___.___.___.1 to ___.___.___.254	254

Materials Required

This lab will require the following:

➤ Windows 9x

➤ A lab workgroup size of 2–4 students

➤ The IP address from your lab workstation

➤ Each computer must have an NIC installed and functioning properly.

Estimated completion time: **45 minutes**

ACTIVITY

Converting binary octets to decimal format:

1. In Table 7-4, convert each of the binary numbers to decimal. The first one has been done for you.

Table 7-4   Converting binary to decimal

	Binary	128	64	32	16	8	4	2	1	Decimal
Example	00110000	0	0	1	1	0	0	0	0	32 + 16 = 48
1st Octet	11111111									
2nd Octet	00011010									
3rd Octet	10111010									
4th Octet	00000001									

2. Using information from Table 7-4, write the decimal value of each octet in dot notation on the line provided. The result will be an IP address, for example: 132.7.3.1.

_____

Identifying address information for your computer:

3. Click **Start**, click **Run**, type **winipcfg**, and then click **OK**.

4. Click the **Adapter** list arrow, and then select your NIC. You will see the IP address information on your screen. (Your screen should resemble Figure 7-1.)

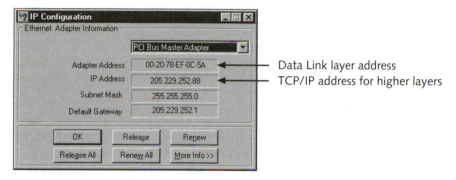

Figure 7-1   Use the Windows 9x WinIPcfg utility to display a PC's IP address and MAC address

5. Review the information provided by the IP configuration utility, and then write your computer's IP address on the line provided.

_____

6. Review the information provided by the IP configuration utility, and then write your computer's MAC address on the line provided.

_____

7. Click **More Info**.

8. Review the information provided by the IP configuration utility, and then write down the IP address of your computer's primary DNS server.

_____

9. Review the information provided by the IP configuration utility, and then write down the IP address of your computer's secondary DNS server.

_____

10. Click **OK**.

Convert your decimal IP addresses to binary:

1. Complete Table 7-5 with the IP address from your lab workstation, and then calculate the binary equivalent for each octet.

Table 7-5   Converting decimal to binary

	Decimal	128	64	32	16	8	4	2	1	Binary
Example	48	0	0	1	1	0	0	0	0	00110000
1st Octet										
2nd Octet										
3rd Octet										
4th Octet										

2. Using information from Table 7-5, write your binary IP address in dot notation on the line provided, for example: 10000100.00000111.00000011.00000001.

_____

Understanding IP address classes:

1. Using Table 7-3 as a reference, write the IP address class name for each of the following addresses:

15.15.15.18 _____

129.128.24.18 _____

132.64.8.18 _____

200.118.24.10 _____

204.24.8.16 _____

204.24.16.24 _____

Certification Objectives:

Objectives for the i-Net+ Exam:

➤ Understand and be able to describe the infrastructure needed to support an Internet client.

➤ Understand and be able to describe the core components of the Internet infrastructure.

Review Questions

1. The binary number 11000001 is equal to 129 in decimal format. True or False?

2. The binary number 00001 is equal to 2 in decimal format. True or False?

3. Each octet contains 4 bits. True or False?

4. An IP address is a 32-bit address. True or False?

5. 15.8.132.99 is an example of a class A network address. True or False?

6. An octet is another name for an IP address. True or False?

LAB 7.2 DOCUMENTING AN IP NETWORK

Objectives

The objective of this lab is to document an IP network, develop an understanding of how TCP/IP routing occurs on the Internet, and become more familiar with your lab environment.

To understand routing, you must be familiar with the term "gateway." A gateway is any device that provides network access to other networks. In the case of a TCP/IP network, a gateway typically is a router or brouter that is used to route data between networks. The term "default gateway" refers to a TCP/IP gateway that is employed when a node is unsure of how to route a packet or packets.

After completing this lab, you will be able to:

➤ Understand routing and how it is used in networks

Materials Required

This lab will require the following:

➤ Windows 2000 or NT

➤ A lab workgroup size of 4 students

➤ At least one router

➤ Instructor should have at least one router configured for use on the computer lab network.

➤ Instructor should have at least one DNS server configured for use on the computer lab network.

➤ Instructor will provide five IP addresses that the student will use for the routing activity. These addresses are the destination addresses used in the following activity. The IP addresses do not need to exist within the computer lab. Students will provide routing information for each of these IP addresses.

Estimated completion time: **45 minutes**

ACTIVITY

Adding your computer to the network diagram:

Figure 7-2 contains a network diagram. You will fill in this diagram with information that you obtain in this lab.

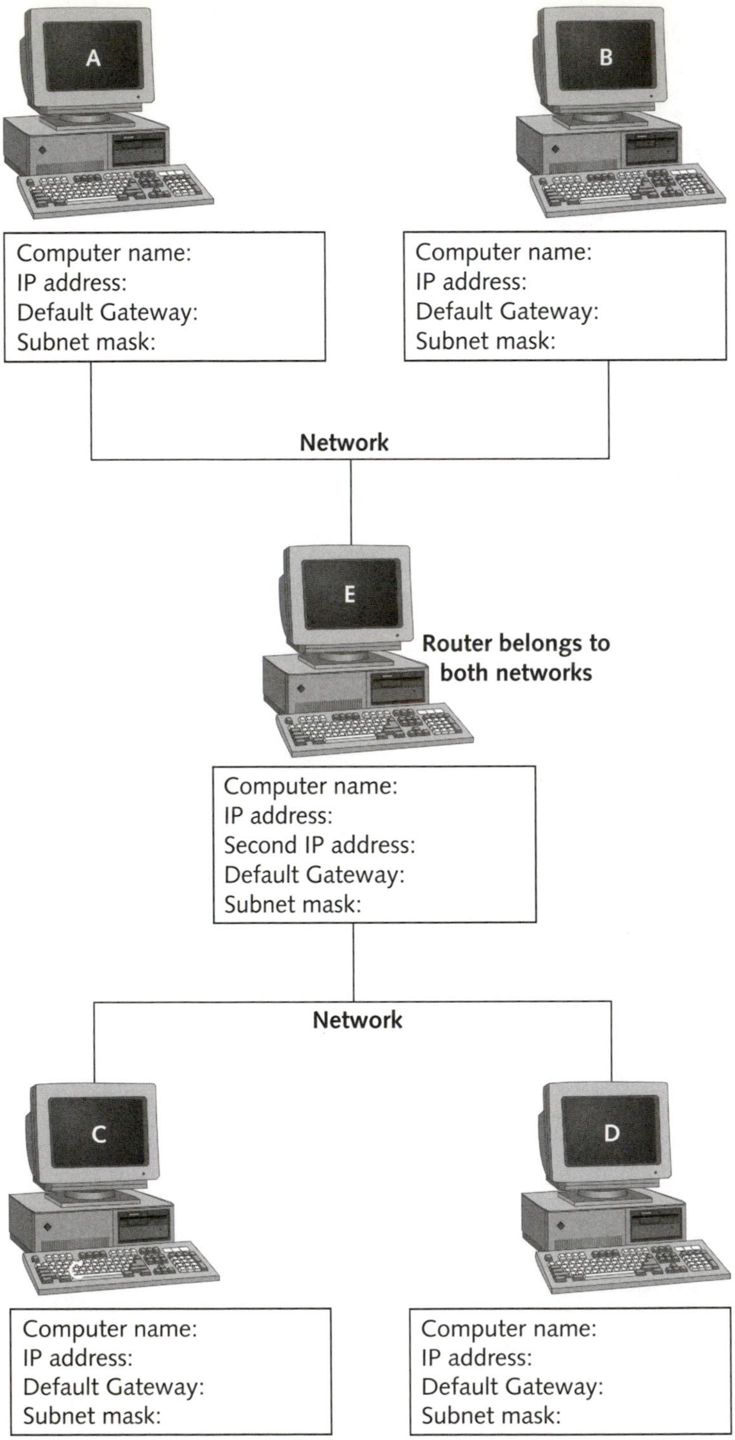

Computer name:
IP address:
Default Gateway:
Subnet mask:

Computer name:
IP address:
Default Gateway:
Subnet mask:

Network

Router belongs to both networks

Computer name:
IP address:
Second IP address:
Default Gateway:
Subnet mask:

Network

Computer name:
IP address:
Default Gateway:
Subnet mask:

Computer name:
IP address:
Default Gateway:
Subnet mask:

Figure 7-2   Two networks using TCP/IP connected by a router

1. Click **Start**, and then click **Run**.

2. Type **command**, and then click **OK**. You have opened the command window on your screen.

3. Type **net name**, and then press **Enter**. This will display your workstation's name in the command window.

4. Write the name of your computer in the Computer A box of Figure 7-2.

5. Type **ipconfig**, and then press **Enter**. This will display your workstation's IP address information.

6. Write the IP address, subnet mask, and default gateway in the Computer A box of Figure 7-2.

7. Type **exit**, and then press **Enter**.

Completing the lab network diagram:

1. Fill in the remaining three computers in your diagram with the information provided by your lab partners.

2. Use the router information provided by your instructor to complete the diagram.

3. Label the router in the diagram as **Default Gateway**.

Routing in the computer lab network diagram:

1. Write down the first destination IP address supplied by your instructor.

   _____

2. If you sent a message from your computer to this destination IP address, how would the message travel through the network?

   _____
   _____
   _____
   _____
   _____
   _____

3. Write down the second destination IP address supplied by your instructor.

   _____

4. If you sent a message from your computer to this destination IP address, how would the message travel through the network?

   _____
   _____
   _____
   _____
   _____

5. Write down the third destination IP address supplied by your instructor.

_____

6. If you sent a message from your computer to this destination IP address, how would the message travel through the network?

_____
_____
_____
_____
_____
_____

7. Write down the fourth destination IP address supplied by your instructor.

_____

8. If you sent a message from your computer to this destination IP address, how would the message travel through the network?

_____
_____
_____
_____
_____
_____

9. Write down the fifth destination IP address supplied by your instructor.

_____

10. If you sent a message from your computer to this destination IP address, how would the message travel through the network?

_____
_____
_____
_____
_____
_____

Certification Objectives:

Objectives for the i-Net+ Exam:

➤ Understand and be able to describe the core components of the Internet infrastructure.

➤ Identify when to use various diagnostic tools for resolving Internet problems.

➤ Describe various hardware and software connection devices and when to use them.

Review Questions

1. A default gateway is used to route data from one network to another. True or False?

2. Every computer on a network actively routes data by examining each packet and passing it to the correct computer. True or False?

3. Default gateways are typically implemented using active hubs. True or False?

4. The ipconfig utility will display information about a computers name and IP address. True or False?

5. If two computers reside on the same IP network, they can often communicate without sending data to the default gateway. True or False?

6. Describe how to add a third network to Figure 7-5 using only existing equipment.

_____

_____

_____

_____

_____

7

LAB 7.3 UNDERSTANDING THE DOMAIN NAME SERVICE (DNS)

Objectives

The objective of this lab is to familiarize you with how Domain Name Service (DNS) functions and how it is used on the Internet.

A DNS server (Domain Name Server) maintains a database of host computers and their IP addresses so that when a client makes a request by the host name, the DNS server can find the IP address for that host. One example of a DNS client request is when someone types a URL into a web browser. The first thing a web browser will do is send a request to the configured DNS server and try to resolve the DNS name to an IP address. For this reason, the DNS name resolution process is critical to TCP/IP communication.

After completing this lab, you will be able to:

➤ Define the term DNS

➤ Describe the difference between forward and reverse lookup

➤ Use the nslookup utility

➤ Describe the relationship between a DNS name and an IP address

Materials Required

This lab will require the following:

> ➤ Windows 2000 or NT

> ➤ A lab workgroup size of 2–4 students

> ➤ Microsoft Internet Explorer 5 or later installed on each lab computer

> ➤ Each student must have the ability to use the nslookup utility.

> ➤ The instructor must provide five domain names that can be used to complete the following activates. Each lab workgroup will complete a forward and a reverse lookup for each domain name.

Estimated completion time: **45 minutes**

ACTIVITY

Using nslookup to determine an IP address (forward lookup):

1. Click **Start**, and then click **Run**.

2. Type **command**, and then click **OK**.

3. Type **nslookup www.microsoft.com**, and then press **Enter**.

4. Write the domain name and IP address returned by nslookup on the line provided.

_____

5. When you are finished, type **exit** and then press **Enter**.

6. Complete Steps 1–5 for each domain name provided by your instructor. Record the results on the lines provided below.

_____
_____
_____
_____
_____

Using nslookup to determine a domain name (reverse lookup):

1. Click **Start**, and then click **Run**.

2. Type **command**, and then click **OK**.

3. Type **nslookup xx.xx.xxx.xxx** (where x's are one of the IP addresses returned from the previous activity), and then press **Enter**.

4. Does the name returned by nslookup match the name you recorded for that IP address in the previous activity? Why or why not?

_____

_____

_____

_____

_____

Certification Objectives:

Objectives for the i–Net+ Exam:

➤ Understand and be able to describe the infrastructure needed to support an Internet client.

➤ Understand and be able to describe the use of Internet domain names and DNS.

➤ Identify when to use various diagnostic tools for resolving Internet problems.

Review Questions

1. A name server can provide IP address to host name resolution. True or False?

2. All valid Internet host names must be associated with at least one IP address. True or False?

3. The nslookup utility can be used to resolve a host name to an IP address via DNS server. True or False?

4. A valid DNS sever must be available in order for the nslookup utility to function properly. True or False?

5. The primary role of a Name Server is to provide name resolution. True or False?

6. Describe the difference between forward and reverse IP address lookup.

_____

_____

_____

_____

_____

CHAPTER EIGHT

INTERNET CLIENTS

Labs included in this chapter

➤ Lab 8.1 Install an Internal Modem, Dial-Up Networking, and Drivers

➤ Lab 8.2 Connecting a PC to a Local Area Network (LAN)

➤ Lab 8.3 Installing Software Updates and Understanding the Web Browser Cache

i-Net+ Exam Objectives	
Objectives	**Lab**
Understand and be able to describe the infrastructure needed to support an Internet client.	8.1, 8.2, 8.3
Understand and be able to describe the capabilities of popular remote access protocols.	8.1
Identify when to use various diagnostic tools for resolving Internet problems.	8.2
Understand and be able to describe the concept of caching and its implications.	8.3
Use/configure Web browsers and other Internet/intranet clients, and be able to describe their use to others.	8.3
Update client software.	8.3

LAB 8.1 INSTALL AN INTERNAL MODEM, DIAL-UP NETWORKING, AND DRIVERS

Objectives

The objective of this lab is to familiarize you with the installation and configuration of an internal modem. During this activity you will install the hardware and software required to use an internal modem with the Windows 9x operating system.

A modem driver ensures proper communication between the operating system and the modem's hardware. After you have the modem driver working, you can configure a dialer, which is a Windows 9x object that contains settings for a particular dial-up connection, such as phone numbers, IP address, and allowed protocols. In Windows 9x, you can create and configure multiple dialers, each of which can contain a different configuration.

After completing this lab exercise, you will be able to:

➤ Install an internal modem

➤ Install Dial-Up Networking

➤ Install the dial-up adapter

➤ Configure Windows 9x to use a PPP dial-up connection

Materials Required

This lab will require the following:

➤ Windows 9x

➤ A lab workgroup size of 2–4 students

➤ One jumper-configurable PCI or ISA internal modem for each lab workgroup

➤ A screwdriver, a Torx wrench, a grounding strap, and any other tools that may be required to install a modem

➤ An unplugged power cord and proper grounding

➤ Information required to access the CMOS Setup program

➤ The removal of all networking components that might be present

Estimated completion time: **1 hour**

ACTIVITY

Installing a modem:

1. Power off and unplug your lab workstation.

2. Remove the case.

3. Locate an available ISA or PCI slot for the internal modem.

4. Remove any blanks that might be in place.

5. Configure the modem's jumpers to use an available COM port.

6. Gently install the modem into the slot. Be careful not to bend the modem from side to side.

7. Secure the modem with a screw.

8. Plug in the lab workstation.

9. Stand clear of the lab workstation and power it on.

10. Enter the CMOS Setup program.

11. Verify that the modem is not conflicting with an existing COM port.

12. If the modem is conflicting with a COM port, disable the COM port.

13. Save your changes and reboot the PC.

14. Power off your lab workstation.

15. Unplug the power cord.

16. Replace the case.

17. Plug in the power cord.

18. Stand clear of your lab workstation, power it on, and allow it to boot into Windows 9x.

Installing Dial-Up Networking:

1. Power on your lab workstation and allow it to boot into Windows 9*x*.

2. Click **Start**, point to **Settings**, and then click **Control Panel**.

3. Double-click the **Add/Remove Programs** icon.

4. Click the **Windows Setup** tab.

5. In the list of components, double-click **Communications**.

6. Click the **Dial-Up Networking** check box, Your window should look similar to the window shown in Figure 8-1.

8

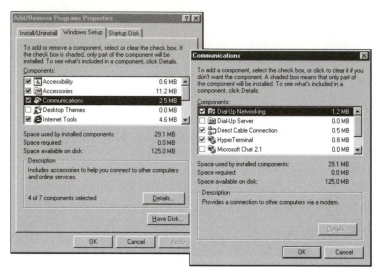

Figure 8-1   Install Dial-Up Networking from the Add/Remove Programs window accessible from the Control Panel

7. Click **OK** to close the Communications dialog box.

8. Click **OK**.

9. If prompted, enter the path to the installation files.

Installing a modem driver:

1. Click **Start**, point to **Settings**, and then click **Control Panel**.

2. Double-click the **Modems** icon.

3. If you are not prompted to install a modem, click **Add**.

4. Click **Next** to have Windows 9x search for a modem.

5. Verify that Windows 9x has detected the correct type of modem. You may have to provide a disk if Windows cannot detect your modem.

6. Click **Next**.

7. Click **Finish**.

8. Click **OK**.

Installing the dial-up adapter:

1. Click the **Start** button, point to **Settings**, and then click **Control Panel**.

2. Double-click the **Network** icon.

3. Click **Add**.

4. In the type of component list, double-click **Client**.

5. Select **Microsoft** from the Manufacturer list.

6. Double-click **Client for Microsoft Networks**.

7. Click **Add**, and then double-click **Adapter** in the Type of Component drop-down list.

8. Select **Microsoft** from the Manufacturer list.

9. In the list of installed network components, double-click **Dial-Up Adapter**.

10. Click **Add**.

11. In the list of network components, double-click **Protocol**.

12. Select **Microsoft** from the Manufacturer list.

13. Click **TCP/IP**. Your window should look similar to the window shown in Figure 8-2.

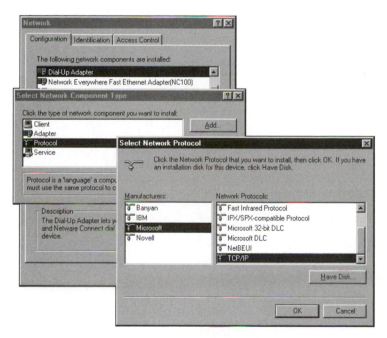

Figure 8-2   Install the TCP/IP protocol

14. Click **OK**.

15. If prompted, enter the path to the installation files.

16. Click **Yes** when prompted to restart your computer.

Creating and configuring a dialer:

1. Double-click the **My Computer** icon.

2. Double-click the **Dial-Up Networking** icon.

3. Double-click **Make New Connection**.

4. Type **Lab Dialer** in the Type a name for the computer you are dialing text box, and then click **Next**.

5. Type **444–4444** in the Telephone Number text box, or type the number of the ISP you will be calling.

6. Click **Next**.

7. Click **Finish**.

8. In the Dial-Up Networking window, right-click the **Lab Dialer** icon, and then click **Properties**.

9. Click the **Server Types** button.

10. Verify that the type of dial-up server is set to the PPP Windows 95, Windows NT 3.5, Internet option, or the PPP:Internet, Windows NT Server, Windows 98 option.

11. Uncheck the **NetBEUI** and **IPX/SPX** check boxes.

12. Click the **TCP/IP Settings** button.

13. Click the **Specify Name Server Addresses** option button.

14. Type the primary DNS address, provided by your instructor or ISP, in the primary DNS text box.

15. Click **OK** to close the TCP/IP Settings dialog box.

16. Click **OK** to close the Server Types dialog box.

17. Click **OK** to close the Lab Dialer dialog box.

Certification Objectives:

Objectives for the i-Net+ Exam:

➤ Understand and be able to describe the infrastructure needed to support an Internet client.

➤ Understand and be able to describe the capabilities of popular remote access protocols.

Review Questions

1. Each dialer on a Windows 9x computer can use a different phone number and protocol. True or False?

2. A dialer can be created using the Make New Connection option in the Dial-up Networking folder. True or False?

3. The Install Modem Driver icon found in Control Panel is used to install a modem driver. True or False?

4. A modem's jumpers are typically used to configure the IRQ and COM port settings for the modem. True or False?

5. The Add New Hardware option in Control Panel can be used to install Dial-Up Networking. True or False?

6. Describe the difference between a Windows 9x dialer and a Windows 9x modem driver.

_____

_____

_____

_____

_____

8

LAB 8.2   CONNECTING A PC TO A LOCAL AREA NETWORK (LAN)

Objectives

The objective of this lab exercise is to provide you with hands-on networking experience in the Windows 9x environment. In particular, you will connect a PC to a LAN.

To effectively work through this lab, you need to know the following facts:

➤ In the networking environment, the term bandwidth refers to the amount of data that can travel through a wire at any one time.

➤ DNS stands for Domain Name System or Domain Name Service. DNS is a database on a top-level domain name server that keeps track of assigned domain names and their corresponding IP addresses.

➤ The ping command is a useful diagnostic tool that can be used to test network connectivity. Ping sends a signal to a remote computer specified using the computer's name or IP address. If the computer is on the network, it will respond; otherwise, the command will time out.

After completing this lab exercise, you will be able to:

➤ Install network interface card drivers

➤ Configure Windows 9x to communicate on a LAN

➤ Share resources in a networked environment

➤ Configure the TCP/IP protocol in the Windows 9x environment

Materials Required

This lab will require the following:

➤ Windows 9x

➤ A lab workgroup size of 2–4 students

➤ A network Interface card installed in each lab workstation

➤ A lab workstation with no networking components installed

➤ A classroom wired for network communication

➤ An IP address for each lab workstation

➤ A computer name for each lab workstation

Estimated completion time: **1 hour**

ACTIVITY

Installing network interface card drivers:

1. Power on your lab workstation and allow it to boot into Windows 9x.

2. Click **Start**, point to **Settings**, and then click **Control Panel**.

3. Double-click the **Network** icon.

4. Click **Add**.

5. In the list of network components, double-click **Client**.

6. In the list of manufacturers, click **Microsoft**.

7. In the list of network clients, double-click **Client for Microsoft Networks**.

8. In the list of manufacturers, click the manufacturer of your network interface card.

9. Double-click the correct NIC driver.

10. Click **Add**.

11. Double-click **Protocol**.

12. In the Manufacturers list, click **Microsoft**.

13. Double-click **TCP/IP**.

14. Click the **Identification** tab.

15. Type the computer name specified by your instructor.

16. Click **OK**.

17. If prompted, enter the path to the installation files.

18. Click **Yes** when you are prompted to restart your computer.

Configuring the TCP/IP protocol:

1. Click the **Start** button, point to **Settings**, and then click **Control Panel**.

2. Double-click the **Network** icon.

3. Double-click **TCP/IP**.

4. Click the **Specify an IP address** option button.

5. Type the IP address issued to your lab workstation.

6. Enter any additional information required by your instructor.

7. Click **OK**.

8. Click **OK**.

9. Click **Yes** when prompted to restart your computer.

Using the PING command to test the network:

1. Click **Start**, point to **Programs**, and then click **MS-DOS Prompt**.

2. Type **PING ###.###.###.###** (where the ###'s represent your lab workstation's IP address).

3. Type **PING ###.###.###.###** (where the ###'s represent the IP address of your neighbor's lab workstation).

4. Close the DOS window.

Enabling resource sharing:

1. Click **Start**, point to **Settings**, and then click **Control Panel**.

2. Double-click the **Network** icon.

3. Click the **File and Print Sharing** option button.

4. Check the **I want to be able to give others access to my files.** and the **I want to be able to allow others to print to my printer(s).** checkboxes to allow the lab workstations to share resources.

5. Click **OK**, click **OK**, and then click **Yes** when prompted to restart your computer.

Sharing your C: drive:

1. Double-click the **My Computer** icon.

2. Right-click the icon for your C drive, and then click **Properties**.

3. Click the **Sharing** tab.

4. Click the **Shared As** option button.

5. Click the **Full** option button.

6. Click **OK**.

Connecting to a shared resource:

1. Right-click the **Network Neighborhood** icon, and then click **Map Network Drive**.

2. Select **G** from the Drive drop-down list.

3. Type **COMPUTERNAME\SHARENAME** in the path text box (where *COMPUTERNAME\SHARENAME* describes your neighbor's computer).

4. Click **OK**.

Certification Objectives:

Objectives for the i-Net+ Exam:

➤ Understand and be able to describe the infrastructure needed to support an Internet client.

➤ Identify when to use various diagnostic tools for resolving Internet problems.

Review Questions

1. The Network option in Control Panel can be used to configure networking in Windows 9x. True or False?

2. Ping is used to test network connectivity by sending packets of data to a remote IP address. True or False?

3. The phrase "mapping a drive" describes assigning a logic drive letter to a shared network resource. True or False?

4. Darrell can share his C drive by right-clicking the My Computer icon and clicking the Share My C Drive option. True or False?

5. Where do you specify a computer and workgroup name in Windows 9x?

_____

_____

_____

_____

_____

6. Describe how to change a computer's IP address in Windows 9x.

_____

_____

_____

_____

_____

LAB 8.3 INSTALLING SOFTWARE UPDATES AND UNDERSTANDING THE WEB BROWSER CACHE

Objectives

The objective of this lab exercise is to provide you with hands-on experience installing software updates and service packs in the Windows 9x environment. You will also learn how to configure web cache settings using Internet Explorer.

Before beginning this lab, you need to know the following facts:

➤ A software update, sometimes referred to as a patch, is a fix for a known software defect, and is typically downloadable from the manufacturer's web site. A service pack, also called a service release, is a group of fixes or patches that are bundled into one large update and that are generally downloaded from the manufacturer's web site.

➤ The Windows Update utility connects your computer to the Microsoft web site and automatically compares your computer's configuration, including updates and service packs, to a list of known updates from the Microsoft web site. If updates or service packs are identified that you have not installed, the Windows Update Web site enables you to download and install the latest updates.

➤ Cache is a place where a program holds frequently used data to improve performance. Internet Explorer caches web pages to the hard drive and Netscape Navigator caches Web pages to the hard drive and to memory.

After completing this lab exercise, you will be able to:

➤ Install updates and service packs in the Windows 9x environment

➤ Define the term cache

➤ Describe the concept of caching and its implications

Materials Required

This lab will require the following:

➤ Windows 9x

➤ A lab workgroup size of 2–4 students

➤ A connection to the Internet

➤ Internet Explorer 5.0 or later version

8

Estimated completion time: **30 minutes**

ACTIVITY

Installing updates and service packs using Windows Update:

1. Click **Start**, and then click **Windows Update**. If you are prompted by a security warning, click **Yes**.

2. Click the **Product Updates** link on the Microsoft web page. If you are prompted by a security warning, click **Yes**.

3. Scroll down in your browser window to view the updates available for your computer. By default, the Critical Package Updates will be selected. Choose additional updates to install by clicking the check box next to the package name. When you have finished making your selections, click the **Download** button at the top of the page.

4. Click **Start Download**.

5. Click **Yes** to accept the license agreement.

6. If prompted to restart your computer, click **Yes**.

7. Close the Internet Explorer browser window, if necessary.

Configure Internet Explorer web cache disk space:

1. From your Windows desktop, double-click **Internet Explorer**.

2. Click **Tools** on the menu bar, and then click **Internet Options**.

3. Click **Settings**.

4. Using the backspace key, erase the number in the megabytes textbox, and then type **1**.

5. Click **OK**.

6. In the Internet Options dialog box, click **OK**.

7. Close the Internet Explorer browser window.

8. On the lines provided, describe how the previous steps will affect your Web browser.

   _____

   _____

Disable Internet Explorer web cache:

1. From your Windows desktop, double-click **Internet Explorer**.

2. Click **Tools**, and then click **Internet Options**.

3. Click **Settings**.

4. Drag the **Disk Space** slide bar to the right until it points between the first and second lines.

5. Click the **Never** toggle button, and then click **OK**.

6. In the Internet Options dialog box, click **OK**.

7. On the lines provided, describe how the previous steps will affect your Web browser.

   _____

   _____

8. Close your browser.

Enable automatic Internet Explorer web cache:

1. From your Windows desktop, double-click **Internet Explorer**.

2. Click **Tools**, and then click **Internet Options**.

3. Click **Settings**.

4. Click the **Automatically** toggle button, and then click **OK**.

5. In the Internet Options dialog box, click **OK**.

Certification Objectives:

Objectives for the i-Net+ Exam:

➤ Understand and be able to describe the concept of caching and its implications.

➤ Understand and be able to describe the infrastructure needed to support an Internet client.

➤ Use/configure Web browsers and other Internet/intranet clients, and be able to describe their use to others.

➤ Update client software.

Review Questions

1. The Windows Update utility is designed to provide software updates for the Windows operating system and other Microsoft applications. True or False?

2. A service pack typically contains fixes for multiple defects. True or False?

3. Caching more than five web pages at a time will significantly decrease web browser performance. True or False?

8

4. Caching a web page generally improves web browser performance. True or False?

5. Microsoft Internet Explorer caches web pages in memory and to the hard disk, whereas Netscape Navigator caches web pages only to the hard disk. True or False?

6. Amanda told you that she has added a new image to her web site. After connecting to her web site using Internet Explorer 5.0, you do not see the new image she described. On the lines provided, explain how your browser's web cache settings could cause this problem, and the steps you could take to view Amanda's updated page containing the new image.

_____

_____

_____

_____

_____

CHAPTER NINE

SOLVING CLIENT PROBLEMS

Labs included in this chapter

➤ Lab 9.1 Windows 98 Advanced Utilities

➤ Lab 9.2 Managing Windows 98 User Accounts and User Profiles

➤ Lab 9.3 Troubleshooting Web Sites

i-Net+ Exam	
Objectives:	Lab
Understand and be able to describe the infrastructure needed to support an Internet client.	9.1, 9.2
Assist in the administration of Internet/intranet sites.	9.3

LAB 9.1 WINDOWS 98 ADVANCED UTILITIES

Objectives

The objective of this lab is to provide you with hands-on experience using various utilities in the Windows 98 environment. Mastering the use of these utilities will improve your ability to troubleshoot and resolve Windows 98 client problems.

The Registry is an internal Windows database that stores configuration information about Windows 9x user preferences and software settings. The Windows Registry Checker makes a backup copy of the Registry each day that Windows 98 is successfully started. It can also be manually invoked at the command prompt by typing scanreg.

Scan Disk is a Windows and DOS utility that fixes file system errors on a hard drive. The Scan Disk utility can also be manually invoked at the command prompt by typing scandisk.

The Disk Defragmenter is a Windows and DOS utility that reorganizes files on a hard drive so that files are written to the drive in contiguous segments. When files are written in contiguous segments, Windows can read them into memory faster, which results in a performance increase for the user. The Disk Defragmenter can also be manually invoked at the command prompt by typing defrag.

After completing this lab exercise, you will be able to:

➤ Back up a Windows 98 Registry using the Registry Checker

➤ Restore a Windows 98 Registry using the Registry Checker

➤ Use the Windows Disk Cleanup utility to remove temporary files

➤ Use the Scan Disk utility to repair errors found on your hard drive

➤ Use the Disk Defragmenter to defragment your hard drive

Materials Required

This lab will require the following:

➤ Windows 98

➤ A lab workgroup size of 2–4 students

Estimated completion time: **1 hour**

ACTIVITY

Back up the Windows 98 Registry:

1. Click **Start**, click **Run**, type **command**, and then click **OK**.

2. Type **scanreg**, and then press **Enter**.

3. Click **Yes** when you are prompted to back up the system registry again.

4. Click **OK** when the backup has completed.

5. Type **exit**, and then press **Enter**.

Restoring the Windows 98 Registry:

1. Click **Start**, click **Shut Down**, click **Restart**, and then click **OK**.

2. When your computer begins to reboot, press the **F8** key. A menu will appear.

If you are having trouble accessing the Windows 98 Startup menu, try slowly and repeatedly pressing F8 after POST has completed the keyboard check.

3. At the Microsoft Windows Startup menu, use your down arrow key to select **5 Command prompt Only**.

4. Press **Enter**.

5. At the command prompt, type **scanreg /restore**, and then press **Enter**.

6. Use the down arrow key to select the newest backup of your Registry, and then press **Enter**.

7. After the Registry has been successfully restored, you will be prompted to restart your computer by pressing **Enter**.

Using the Scan Disk utility:

1. Double-click **My Computer**.

2. Right-click your **C:** drive, and then click **Properties**.

3. Click the **Tools** tab, and then click the **Check Now** button. A window similar to Figure 9-1 will be displayed.

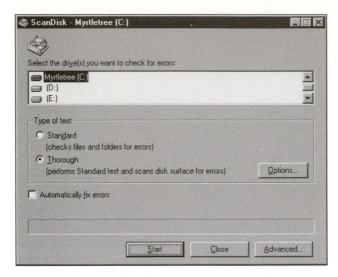

Figure 9-1 Use ScanDisk to scan the hard drive for errors and repair those errors

4. Click **Start** to begin the Scan Disk utility.

5. If you are prompted to repair an error, click **Repair the error**, and then click **OK**.

6. Click **Close** in the Scan Disk Results dialog box and in the Scan Disk window when the Scan Disk utility has finished checking your hard drive.

Using the Disk Defragmenter utility:

1. While still on the Tools tab, click the **Defragment Now** button. Depending on the size and fragmentation of your disk drive, the procedure may run for several hours.

2. If you do not want to wait for this program to finish, click **Stop**.

3. When the Disk Defragmenter has finished, click **Close**.

4. In the C: Properties dialog box, click **OK**.

Using the Disk Cleanup utility:

1. Double-click **My Computer**.

2. Right-click your **C:** drive, and then click **Properties**.

3. Click the **Disk Cleanup** button.

4. Place a check mark in the **Temporary Internet Files** check box.

5. Place a check mark in the **Downloaded Program Files** check box.

6. Place a check mark in the **Recycle Bin** check box.

7. Place a check mark in the **Temporary files** check box.

8. Click **OK**, and then click **Yes**.

Certification Objectives:

Objectives for the i-Net+ Exam:

➤ Understand and be able to describe the infrastructure needed to support an Internet client.

Review Questions

1. The Disk Cleanup utility is used to delete unwanted temporary files and restore the Windows Registry. True or False?

2. Typing regchk at a command prompt will start the Windows 98 Registry Checker. True or False?

3. The Registry Checker can both back up and restore the Windows 98 Registry. True or False?

4. A file is considered fragmented when it is not saved on the hard drive in one contiguous segment. True or False?

5. The Scan Disk utility can identify and repair file system errors found on a hard drive. True or False?

6. Martha has contacted you because her Windows 98 computer has been gradually getting slower and slower over the last year. You inspect the properties of her hard drive and discover that she only has 10 MB of free disk space. Which utility from this lab could you use to increase the performance of Martha's computer and provide her with more free disk space?

_____

_____

_____

_____

_____

9

LAB 9.2 MANAGING WINDOWS 98 USER ACCOUNTS AND USER PROFILES

Objectives

The objective of this lab exercise is to provide you with hands-on experience managing Windows 98 user accounts and user profiles.

In its simplest form, a user account is a unique user name and password typically assigned to an individual. A user profile is a snapshot of a user account environment that includes the user's desktop configuration, Start menu shortcuts, and some application settings. Each time a user logs into Windows 9x, the operating system automatically accesses the user's profile and displays his or her saved settings. In the case of a new user, Windows automatically creates a profile for the user based on a default user profile.

After completing this lab exercise, you will be able to:

➤ Create a Windows 98 user

➤ Change a user's password

➤ Delete a Windows 98 user

➤ Define and describe a user profile

➤ Install a patch using Windows Update

Materials Required

This lab will require the following:

➤ Windows 9x

➤ A lab workgroup size of 2–4 students

➤ Microsoft Internet Explorer 5 or later

➤ A connection to the Internet

➤ Only one configured user per workstation

Estimated completion time: **45 minutes**

ACTIVITY

Creating the student01 user account:

1. Click **Start**, click **Settings**, and then click **Control Panel**.

2. Double-click **Users**.

3. Click **Next**. If you already have multiple users, you need to click **New User** and **Next** before continuing.

4. Type **student01**, and then click **Next**.

5. Type **password** in both the Password: and the Confirm password: text boxes, and then click **Next**.

6. Check the **Desktop folder Documents menu**, **Start Menu**, **Favorites folder**, **Downloaded Web pages**, and **My Documents folder** check boxes.

7. Click the **Create new items to save disk space** option button, and then click **Next**.

8. Click **Finish**.

9. When prompted to restart your computer, click **Yes**.

Log in to the student01 account:

1. After your computer has rebooted, type **student01** in the User name: text box, if necessary.

2. Type **password** in the Password text box, and then click **OK** to log in. Remember that passwords are case-sensitive.

Creating the student02 user account:

1. Click **Start**, click **Settings**, and then click **Control Panel**.

2. Double-click **Users**, and then click **New User**.

3. Click **Next**.

4. Type **student02**, and then click **Next**.

5. Type **password** in both the Password: and the Confirm password: text boxes, and then click **Next**.

6. Check the **Desktop folder Documents menu**, **Start Menu**, **Favorites folder**, **Downloaded Web pages**, and **My Documents folder** check boxes.

7. Click the **Create new items to save disk space** option button, and then click **Next**.

8. Click **Finish**.

9. Click **Close**.

10. Close the Control Panel window.

11. Click **Start**, and then click **Logoff student01**.

12. Click **Yes**.

Log in to the student02 account:

1. Type **student02** in the User name: text box.

2. Type **password** in the Password: text box, and then click **OK** to log in. Remember that passwords are case-sensitive.

Understanding user profiles:

1. Right-click a blank portion of the desktop, point to **New**, and then click **Folder**.

2. Type **myfolder**, and then press **Enter**.

3. Click **Start**, click **Logoff student02**, and then click **Yes**.

4. In the Network Logon dialog box, type the user name and password for student01, and then click **OK**.

5. Does the myfolder folder that you created on the desktop of student02 appear on the desktop of student01? Why or why not?

_____

_____

_____

_____

_____

Delete a user:

1. Click **Start**, click **Settings**, and then click **Control Panel**.

2. Double-click **Users**.

3. Click **student02**, and then click **Delete**.

4. Click **Yes** to confirm the deletion of the user.

5. Click **Close** when you have finished.

Change a user's password:

1. While still in the Control Panel, double-click **Passwords**.

2. Click the **Change Windows Password** button, and then click **OK**.

3. In the Old password: text box, type **password**.

4. In the New password: text box, type **pass2**.

5. In the Confirm new password: text box, type **pass2** again.

6. Click **OK**.

7. Click **OK** when after the change has been completed.

8. Click **Close** when finished.

9. Close the Control Panel.

Certification Objectives:

Objectives for the i-Net+ Exam:

➤ Understand and be able to describe the infrastructure needed to support an Internet client.

Review Questions

1. A user's password can be changed in Windows 98 by clicking the Start button, Settings, Control Panel, and Passwords. True or False?

2. Each user account has one user name and one password. True or False?

3. All users using Windows NT and Windows 2000 have their own user profiles, but all users using Windows 98 must share one user profile. True or False?

4. Desktop colors, wallpaper, screen savers, and computer name settings are all stored in a user's profile. True or False?

5. A Windows 98 user can be deleted only when the computer is in DOS mode. True or False?

6. The following users exist on Jonathon's Windows 98 computer:

   - John
   - Kathy
   - Robert
   - Reema
   - Verbus
   - Charles
   - Henry
   - Erik
   - Darrell
   - Dale

   Robert now has his own computer and Henry has quit, so Jonathon wants to remove their profiles from his computer. Verbus has forgotten his password, so Jonathon also needs to reset his password to a temporary password of changeme.

   On the lines provided, describe the steps Jonathon needs to take to complete all his administrative tasks.

   _____
   _____
   _____
   _____
   _____

LAB 9.3 TROUBLESHOOTING WEB SITES

Objectives

The objective of this lab exercise is to provide you with hands-on experience troubleshooting web sites. Troubleshooting is an essential part of working with computers and web sites. You will expand on what you already know and familiarize yourself with common Web site error messages.

While you design and troubleshoot Web sites, you will encounter web site error messages. These messages will help you identify and resolve common problems. Table 9-1 lists some common error messages.

Table 9-1   Browser error messages

Message	Meaning
Bad File Request	An online form or the HTML code for an online form has an error.
Failed DNS Lookup	The web site's URL couldn't be translated into a valid IP address.
Helper Application Not Found	You have attempted to download a file that needs a helper application, and the browser cannot find it.
Not Found	The page that the hyperlink points to no longer exists.
Site Unavailable	One of several things can cause this message: either too many users are trying to access the site, the site is down for maintenance, there is "noise" on the line, or the site no longer exists. Typing the wrong address can also produce this message.

Sometimes when a browser displays an error message to the user, it does not indicate a status code. Table 9-2 lists examples of errors that do not provide a status code.

Table 9-2   HTTP status code error messages

Code	Meaning
200	Request completed successfully.
201	Data sent, request was a POST.
202	Request accepted, but results unknown.
204	Request fulfilled, but no new information sent to client.
301	Data request has been moved. Server should provide client with new URL.
302	Data found at different URL. Server should provide client with correct URL.
303	Available at different URL, should be retrieved using GET.
304	Request contained **if-modified-since field**. Server indicating file not modified since the date specified, server will not resend the requested document.
400	Requested syntax wrong.
401	The request included an **Authorization** field, but the client (browser) did not supply one.
403	Request for a file that is presently set to forbidden, so the file can't be sent. A browser sometimes reports this status as "Connection Refused by Host".
404	Server can't find the requested URL. Frequently indicates user made a typo in entering the URL string.
405	Server didn't understand the METHOD supplied by the client.
406	Resource found, but not sent. Type of resource incompatible based on information passed between server and client.
408	Client did not produce the request before server timed out.
410	Resource no longer available, server has no forwarding URL.
500	Unfortunately, this error can mean almost anything and will frequently halt execution of a CGI script dead in its tracks. Usually the only message you will see is "Server encountered an internal error and can't continue."

Table 9-2   (continued)

Code	Meaning
501	Server does not support the method being requested. For CGI scripts, a 501 error may mean the server isn't set up to support CGI scripts outside their designation sub-directory. Therefore the method (typically POST) fails since it isn't supported in other directories.
502	Server attempted to retrieve resource from another server or gateway with this secondary server failing to return a valid response on the calling server.
503	Server is too busy and unavailable to process the request. Server may send a special header (called a Retry-After header) to the client that specifies how long the client should wait before trying again.
504	Similar to error #502, but secondary server timed-out before the request could be completed.
505	HTTP version not supported.

Table 9-2 contains a list of HTTP status codes and their meanings. HTTP status codes are three-digit numbers that are generated by the server based on HTTP standards described in RFC 2068, 2616, 2816 and 2817. The codes can be grouped by their general meanings. Codes with numbers 200–299 indicate that a successful transaction took place. Codes numbered 300–399 indicate redirection. Numbers 400–499 are reserved for error messages that indicate the client created a problem. The last range of codes, 500–599, are used to indicate the server has a problem or cannot fulfill the client request.

After completing this lab exercise, you will be able to:

➤ Identify and resolve common web-related error messages

➤ Classify and interpret HTTP error code ranges

➤ Use and be able to describe web site error handling

Materials Required

This lab will require the following:

➤ Windows 9x

➤ A lab workgroup size of 2–4 students

➤ Microsoft Outlook Express 5 or later

➤ A connection to the Internet

➤ One classroom web server

➤ Prior to beginning this lab, the instructor must generate five URLs using the classroom web server. Each generated URL will display an error messages. For example, the instructor could provide an invalid URL to generate the HTTP 404 error message. Only messages found in Table 9-1 or Table 9-2 can be used for this lab.

Estimated completion time: 30 minutes

ACTIVITY

Identifying common web-related error messages for URL #1:

1. Double-click the **Internet Explorer** icon on your desktop.

2. In the Address bar, type the URL provided by your instructor, and then press **Enter**.

3. Record the error message on the line provided.

_____

4. Using the information provided in Tables 9-1 and 9-2, determine the likely cause of this error message and one possible solution.

_____
_____
_____
_____
_____

5. Repeat Steps 2–4 for each of the remaining URLs.

6. For URL #2, write down the error message and likely cause:

_____
_____
_____
_____

7. For URL #3, write down the error message and likely cause:

_____
_____
_____
_____

8. For URL #4, write down the error message and likely cause:

_____
_____
_____
_____

9. For URL #5, write down the error message and likely cause:

_____
_____
_____
_____

Certification Objectives:

Objectives for the i-Net+ Exam:

➤ Assist in the administration of Internet/intranet sites.

Review Questions

1. If a web server returns an HTTP code in the 200 range, the transaction was probably successful. True or False?

2. An HTTP response code of 404 means that the requested web page was not found on the web server. True or False?

3. If the word "forbidden" appears in an error message, you may not have the appropriate permissions to access the page you requested. True or False?

4. An HTTP response of 500 usually means that the requested web page is missing from the web server. True or False?

5. After uploading a new web page to your site, a user calls and says that every time he attempts to access the web page using a hyperlink, his browsers reports a "File not Found" error. From your browser you can type the URL into the Address bar and view the web page. Assuming that there are no web server or network problems, what is the most likely reason the user cannot access the web page?

6. After reading the information provided in Tables 9-1 and 9-2, what error message would you receive if the web server you were trying to access didn't have a valid DNS entry?

9

WEB PROGRAMMING AND RELATED TOOLS

Labs included in this chapter

➤ Lab 10.1 Programming Language Research Project

➤ Lab 10.2 Client-Side Scripting

➤ Lab 10.3 Server-Side Scripting

➤ Lab 10.4 XML and Document Type Definitions (DTDs)

---

i-Net+ Exam Objectives	
Objective	**Lab**
Understand and be able to describe programming-related terms.	10.1, 10.2, 10.3, 10.4
Understand and be able to describe differences between popular client-side and server-side programming languages.	10.1, 10.2, 10.3, 10.4
Create HTML pages	10.4
Identify the common formats used to deliver content to wireless devices.	10.4

Lab 10.1 Programming Language Research Project

Objectives

The objective of this lab is to familiarize you with some of the more commonly used programming languages and technologies found on the Internet.

To successfully complete this lab, you should know that a programming language is a set of commands. Arguments to those commands have a predetermined meaning to the software executing the program. In addition, a script is a list of programming commands stored in a text file to be executed by the operating system or other software.

In programming, an object is anything that is addressed by a program as an entity having properties, attributes, and rules. In contrast, object code is source code that has been compiled into instructions that can be executed by the CPU.

A dynamic linked library (DLL) is a utility program that is called by another program to perform a specific task. For example, a Windows print DLL is called by Microsoft Word to print a document. Thus, Word does not need to manage the printing process. In Windows 9x, DLL files are normally stored in the \Windows\System folder.

An executable file is a program file that has been compiled. It normally has an .exe file extension. In Windows, you execute a program file in Windows Explorer by double-clicking the file.

After completing this lab exercise, you will be able to:

➤ Name and describe various programming languages commonly used on the Internet today

➤ Name and describe various Internet technologies and standards

Materials Required

This lab will require the following:

➤ Windows 9x

➤ A lab workgroup size of 2–4 students

➤ Microsoft Internet Explorer 5 or later installed on each lab computer

➤ Students must have access to a library or the Internet to complete their research.

Estimated completion time: **1 hour**

ACTIVITY

Research using the Internet or the library to answer the following questions about Internet technologies:

1. Is CGI a programming language? If not, what is it?

    _____

    _____

    _____

    _____

    _____

2. In your own words, describe how a CGI program or script typically interacts with a web server.

    _____

    _____

    _____

    _____

    _____

3. On the lines provided, define ISAPI (Internet Server Application Programming Interface).

    _____

    _____

    _____

    _____

    _____

4. On the lines provided, define ASP (Active Server Pages).

    _____

    _____

    _____

    _____

    _____

5. Where does the code for an SSI (Sever-side include) reside?

    _____

    _____

    _____

    _____

10

Research using the Internet or the library to answer the following questions about programming languages:

1. Does Perl support object-oriented programming?

_____

_____

2. When is Perl code typically compiled?

_____

_____

3. Does C support object-oriented programming?

_____

_____

4. When is C code typically compiled?

_____

_____

5. Does C++ support object-oriented programming?

_____

_____

6. When is C++ code typically compiled?

_____

_____

8. Does Java support object-oriented programming?

_____

_____

9. When is Java code typically compiled?

_____

_____

10. Does Visual Basic support object-oriented programming?

_____

_____

11. When is Visual Basic code typically compiled?

_____

_____

12. Does JavaScript support object-oriented programming?

_____

_____

13. When is JavaScript code typically compiled?

_____

_____

14. Does VBScript support object-oriented programming?

_____

_____

15. When is VBScript code typically compiled?

_____

_____

Certification Objectives:

Objectives for the i-Net+ Exam:

➤ Understand and be able to describe programming-related terms.

➤ Understand and be able to describe differences between popular client-side and server-side programming languages.

Review Questions

1. Perl is a scripting language. True or False?

2. A CGI program could be written in C++ code. True or False?

3. The .exe file extension is often used to designate an executable file in the Windows environment. True or False?

4. A DLL is a utility program that can perform a specific task. True or False?

5. CGI and Perl are *not* compatible. True or False?

6. Describe the difference between an object and object code.

_____

_____

_____

_____

_____

LAB 10.2 CLIENT-SIDE SCRIPTING

Objectives

The objective of this lab is to familiarize you with the methods used to create client-side scripts. A client-side script is a script embedded in a web page and is performed by the browser either before the browser displays the page, or when the user clicks a button or performs some other action on the page.

Note that in programming, an argument qualifies or modifies the action that is stated in a command. In addition, a function is a segment of a program that is assigned a name and which sits dormant until called by a command somewhere else in the program to perform a given task. Although the syntax used to declare functions varies from one programming language to another, you can normally identify a function because it uses the following format:

```
FunctionName(arguments_if_any)   {
        commands go here;
}
```

There are many different aspects to the Java language. It is important to understand some of the more common terms and how they are related:

➤ **Java applet**: A small Java program that can be downloaded to a browser and used to perform tasks that the browser cannot, such as add multimedia effects to a web page.

➤ **JavaBean**: A short java program designed to work as a reusable component or object in many different situations.

➤ **Java servlet**: A short Java program embedded in an HTML document.

➤ **Java Speech API (JSAPI)**: An interface developed by Sun and used by Java programs to recognize voice and convert text to speech.

➤ **JScript**: The Microsoft version of JavaScript developed to be used with Internet Explorer.

➤ **JSP**: Java Server Page is a server-side scripting technology that uses Java servlets to control the HTML sent to a client.

After completing this lab exercise, you will be able to:

➤ Describe the advantages of client-side scripting

➤ Write a client-side script

➤ Write a function

➤ Call a function

➤ Describe some of the different terms related to the Java language

Materials Required

This lab will require the following:

➤ Windows 9x

➤ A lab workgroup size of 2–4 students

➤ Microsoft Internet Explorer 5 or later installed on each lab computer

➤ A connection to the Internet for each lab computer

➤ Students must be able to map a network drive to their assigned share on the web server and be provided the UNC path to connect. Student must also be provided the URL to view their personal web directory.

➤ The web server must be configured to use the name "index.html" and the index page for each student's personal web directory.

Estimated completion time: **45 minutes**

ACTIVITY

Setting a default status using a client-side JavaScript:

Do not type the commas or periods at the end of the code that you will type, unless the comma or period is in bold as well.

1. Click **Start**, and then click **Run**.

2. Type **Notepad**, and then press **Enter**.

3. Type **<SCRIPT LANGUAGE="JavaScript">**, and then press **Enter**.

4. Type **defaultStatus = "Welcome to my Index.html web page";**, and then press **Enter**.

5. Type **</SCRIPT>**, and then press **Enter** twice.

6. Type **<HTML>**, and then press **Enter**.

7. Type **<H1>Heading One Text</H1>**, and then press **Enter**.

8. Type **</HTML>**, and then press **Enter**. Your completed web page code should resemble the following:

```
<SCRIPT LANGUAGE="JavaScript">
defaultStatus = "Welcome to my Index.html web  page";
</SCRIPT>

<HTML>
<H1>Heading One Text</H1>
</HTML>
```

9. Save the file as **index.html** and publish it to your personal web directory. If you do not have a personal web directory, save it to your desktop.

10. Close the Notepad window.

11. Open Internet Explorer by double-clicking the **icon** found on your desktop, and then type the URL to your personal web directory. If you do not have a personal web directory, you can simply double-click the index.html file found on your desktop.

10

12. The browser status bar is found in the lower-left corner of the browser window. Did your text appear in the browser status bar? Describe the behavior of the status bar text as you move your cursor over different links and images on the index.html web page.

_____

_____

_____

_____

_____

13. Close Internet Explorer.

Writing the date and time to a dialog box using client-side JavaScript:

1. Click **Start**, and then click **Run**.

2. Type **Notepad**, and then press **Enter**.

3. Click **File**, and then click **Open**.

4. Double-click **index.html**.

5. Move your insertion point to the end of the line that begins with defaultStatus, and then press **Enter** twice.

6. Type **function Greeting() {**, and then press **Enter**. When writing a function, you must first give it a unique name, in this case "Greeting," and then enclose the commands that it will perform in braces {}.

7. Type **alert(Date());**, and then press **Enter**. This is a good example of how functions can be used together. The alert() function is a built-in function that tells a browser to create a small pop-up dialog box containing the string sent to it. In this case, however, we are not calling alert() with a string, but with another function, Date(). This function is another built-in function that returns the date and time on the client computer.

8. Type **}** to end the function, and then press **Enter**.

   Your completed script should appear like this at the top of index.html page:

```
<SCRIPT LANGUAGE="JavaScript">
defaultStatus = "Welcome to my Index.html web page";

function Greeting() {
     alert(Date());
     }
</SCRIPT>
```

9. Using the arrow keys, move your insertion point to the end of the line containing the <HTML> tag, and then press **Enter**.

10. Type **<FORM>**, and then press **Enter**.

11. Type **<INPUT TYPE ="button" VALUE="Current Time" ONCLICK="Greeting()">**, and then press **Enter**. Notice that you have called the Greeting() function here so that when the button is clicked, the Greeting function will be executed. Now you need to test your work.

12. Type **</FORM>**, and then press **Enter**. Your completed web page should resemble the following:

```
<SCRIPT LANGUAGE="JavaScript">
defaultStatus = "Welcome to my Index.html web page";

function Greeting() {
alert(Date());
}

</SCRIPT>

<HTML>
<FORM>
<INPUT TYPE="button" VALUE="Current Time"
  ONCLICK="Greeting()">
</FORM>
<H1>Heading One Text</H1>
</HTML>
```

13. Click **File**, and then click **Save**.

14. Close the Notepad window.

15. Publish index.html to your personal web directory.

16. Open Internet Explorer, and then type the URL to your personal web directory.

17. Click the **Current Time** button and describe the results on the lines provided.

_____

_____

_____

_____

_____

18. Close Internet Explorer.

Certification Objectives:

Objectives for the i-Net+ Exam:

➤ Understand and be able to describe programming-related terms.

➤ Understand and be able to describe differences between popular client-side and server-side programming languages.

10

Review Questions

1. A web browser executes a client-side script. True or False?

2. A function is used to encapsulate a series of commands within a program. True or False?

3. Java does not contain any built-in functions. True or False?

4. A function defined within <SCRIPT> tags cannot be called by an HTML button or form. True or False?

5. A JavaBean is designed to be a reusable portion of Java code. True or False?

6. An applet is a small program that can be downloaded to perform tasks that a browser cannot do. True or False?

LAB 10.3 SERVER-SIDE SCRIPTING

Objectives

The objective of this lab exercise is to familiarize you with ASP and the methods used to create server-side scripts. During this lab exercise, you will continue to build on the index.html page that you created in Lab 10.2.

To effectively use this lab, you should know the following:

➤ A server-side script is a script that is performed by the server before a web page is downloaded to the browser. The script can be stored alone in a CGI file or embedded in a web page.

➤ The most important difference between client-side and server-side scripting is where and when the script is executed. In this lab, none of the script code will be sent to the client computer. The server will execute all the script and then the resulting HTML will be sent to the client.

➤ A cookie is a text file that contains information sent from a web server to a browser. The text file is stored on the user's computer to be retrieved by a web server at a later time.

➤ Commercial sites often use cookies to personalize web pages with information such as: the items a person has purchased or placed in a shopping cart, a user's web site activity, and a visitor's interests to target marketing efforts.

After completing this lab exercise, you will be able to:

➤ Describe the advantages of server-side scripting

➤ Write a server-side script

➤ Compare server-side and client-side scripting

➤ Define the term cookie and describe how cookies are used on the Internet

Materials Required

This lab will require the following:

➤ Windows 9x

➤ A lab workgroup size of 2–4 students

➤ One web server

➤ Microsoft Internet Explorer 5 or later installed on each lab computer

➤ Completion of Lab 10.2

➤ The instructor will assign one directory for each student on an intranet or Internet web server.

➤ Students must be able to map a network drive to their assigned share on the web server and be provided the UNC path to connect. Students must also be provided the URL to view their personal web directory.

➤ The web server must be configured to use the name "index.html" as the index page for each student's personal web directory.

➤ The web server must be configured to support ASP (Active Server Pages).

10

Estimated completion time: **1 hour**

ACTIVITY

Creating the initial Guest Book HTML page:

Do not type the commas or periods at the end of the code that you will type, unless the comma or period is in bold as well.

1. Click **Start**, and then click **Run**.

2. Type **Notepad**, and then click **OK**.

3. Type **<HTML>**, and then press **Enter**.

4. Type **<HEAD>**, and then press **Enter**.

5. Type **<TITLE> My Guest Book</TITLE>**, and then press **Enter**.

6. Type **</HEAD>**, and then press **Enter**.

7. Type **<BODY>**, and then press **Enter**.

8. Type **<H1> Guest Book </H1>**, and then press **Enter**.

9. Type **<P>Welcome to my Guest Book! Please take the time to give me your information so that I know you have visited. Thanks! </P>**, and then press **Enter**.

10. Type **<FORM METHOD="POST" ACTION="gbook.asp">**, and then press **Enter**.

11. Type **First name: <INPUT TYPE="text" SIZE="20" NAME="Fname"><P>**, and then press **Enter** twice.

12. Type **Last name: <INPUT TYPE="text" SIZE="20" NAME="Lname"><P>**, and then press **Enter** twice.

13. Type **Gender: <INPUT TYPE="radio" CHECKED NAME="Gender" VALUE="Male">Male**, and then press **Enter**.

14. Type **<INPUT TYPE ="radio" name="Gender" VALUE="Female">Female<P>**, and then press **Enter** twice.

15. Type **Age: <INPUT TYPE="text" SIZE="3" NAME="Age"><P>**, and then press **Enter** twice.

16. Type **Email Address: <INPUT TYPE="text" SIZE="30" NAME="Email"><P>**, and then press **Enter** twice.

17. Type **<INPUT TYPE="SUBMIT" VALUE="Sign Guest Book"><P>**, and then press **Enter** twice.

18. Type **</FORM>**, and then press **Enter**.

19. Type **</BODY>**, and then press **Enter**.

20. Type **</HTML >**, and then press **Enter**. When you have completed the code for Gbook.html, it should resemble the following example:

```
<HTML>
     <HEAD>
          <TITLE>My Guest Book</TITLE>
     </HEAD>
<BODY>
<H1> Guest Book </H1>
<P>Welcome to my Guest Book! Please take the time to give
me your information so that I know you have visited.Thanks!
</P>
<FORM METHOD="POST" ACTION="gbook.asp">
     First name: <INPUT TYPE="text" SIZE="20" NAME="Fname"><P>
     Last name: <INPUT TYPE="text" SIZE="20" NAME="Lname"><P>
Gender: <INPUT TYPE="radio" CHECKED NAME="Gender"
VALUE="Male">Male
     <INPUT TYPE="radio" name="Gender" VALUE="Female">Female<P>
Age: <INPUT TYPE="text" SIZE="3" NAME="Age"><P>
Email Address: <INPUT TYPE="text" SIZE="30" NAME="Email"><P>
<INPUT TYPE="SUBMIT" VALUE="Sign Guest Book"><P>
</FORM>
</BODY>
</HTML>
```

21. Save the file as **Gbook.html** and publish it to your personal web directory.

22. Using the <A HREF> HTML tag, create a hyperlink on the index.html page you created in Lab 10.2. The hyperlink will connect to Gbook.html and should be named **Guest_Book**. Be sure that the hyperlink is not created within the <FORM> tags.

Creating Gbook.asp and writing to a text file:

1. Click **Start**, and then click **Run**.

2. Type **Notepad**, and then click **OK**.

3. Type **<HTML>**, and then press **Enter**.

4. Type **<HEAD>**, and then press **Enter**.

5. Type **<TITLE>Guest Book Response</TITLE>**, and then press **Enter**.

6. Type **</HEAD>**, and then press **Enter**.

7. Type **<BODY>**, and then press **Enter**.

8. Type **< %=Request.Form("Fname")%>
, and then press **Enter.

9. Type **< %=Request.Form("Lname")%>
, and then press **Enter.

10. Type **< %=Request.Form("Gender")%>
, and then press **Enter.

11. Type **< %=Request.Form("Age")%>
, and then press **Enter.

12. Type **< %=Request.Form("Email")%><P>**, and then press **Enter** twice.

13. Type **< %**, and then press **Enter**. This symbol combination is used to tell the web server that script code follows.

14. Type **Dim filesys**, **guestfile**, and then press **Enter**.

15. Type **Set filesys = CreateObject("Scripting.FileSystemObject")**, and then press **Enter**.

16. Type **Set guestfile = _**, and then press **Enter**.

17. Type **filesys.OpenTextFile(_**

    "*Server_path_to_your_web_directory*\Visitors.txt", **8**, **true)**, where *Server_path_to_your_web_directory* is the actual path to your personal web directory. Your instructor will provide the correct path. Press **Enter**.

18. Type **guestfile.WriteLine Request.Form("Fname")**, and then press **Enter**.

19. Type **guestfile.WriteLine Request.Form("Lname")**, and then press **Enter**.

20. Type **guestfile.WriteLine Request.Form("Gender")**, and then press **Enter**.

21. Type **guestfile.WriteLine Request.Form("Age")**, and then press **Enter**.

22. Type **guestfile.WriteLine Request.Form("Email")**, and then press **Enter**.

10

23. Type **guestfile.Close %>**, and then press **Enter** twice.

24. Type **<H2> The information above has been saved.</H2>**, and then press **Enter**.

25. Type **<A HREF="showgb.asp">View the Guest Book </A>**, and then press **Enter**.

26. Type **</BODY>**, and then press **Enter**.

27. Type **</HTML>**, and then press **Enter**.

28. Save the file with the name **gbook.asp** and publish it to your personal web directory. Your completed web page should look similar to the following:

```
<HTML>
<HEAD>
<TITLE>Guest Book Response</TITLE>
</HEAD>
<BODY>
<%=Request.Form("Fname")%><BR>
<%=Request.Form("Lname")%><BR>
<%=Request.Form("Gender")%><BR>
<%=Request.Form("Age")%><BR>
<%=Request.Form("Email")%><P>

<%
Dim filesys, guestfile
Set filesys = CreateObject("Scripting.FileSystemObject")
Set guestfile = _
"Server_path_to_your_web_directory\Vistors.txt", 8, true)
guestfile.WriteLine Request.Form("Fname")
guestfile.WriteLine Request.Form("Lname")
guestfile.WriteLine Request.Form("Gender")
guestfile.WriteLine Request.Form("Age")
guestfile.WriteLine Request.Form("Email")
guestfile.Close
%>

<H2> The information above has been saved.</H2>
<A HREF="showgb.asp">View the Guest Book </A>
</BODY>
</HTML>
```

29. Use Notepad to create an empty text file named **Vistors.txt** and publish it to your personal web directory location that you specified in the gbook.asp code.

30. Open Internet Explorer, and then type the URL to your index.html page found in your personal web directory.

31. Click the **Guest_Book** link found on the index.html web page.

32. Type the information request by the Guest book page, and then click the **Sign Guest Book** button.

33. Verify that the information you typed appeared in the Visitors.txt file.

34. Close Internet Explorer.

Reading Visitors.txt and writing to the browser window:

1. Click **Start**, and then click **Run**.

2. Type **Notepad**, and then click **OK**.

3. Type **<HTML>**, and then press **Enter**.

4. Type **<HEAD>**, and then press **Enter**.

5. Type **<TITLE>Guest Book Visitors</TITLE>**, and then press **Enter**.

6. Type **</HEAD>**, and then press **Enter**.

7. Type **<BODY>**, and then press **Enter**.

8. Type **The following people have signed my Guest Book<P>**, and then press **Enter** twice.

9. Type **<% Dim filesys, guestfile, First_Name, Last_Name, Gender, Age, Email**, and then press **Enter**.

10. Type **Set filesys = CreateObject("Scripting.FileSystemObject")**, and then press **Enter**.

11. Type **Set guestfile =_**, and then press **Enter**.

12. Type **filesys.OpenTextFile(_ "**

    Server_path_to_your_web_directory\Visitors.txt", 1), where *Server_path_to_your_web_directory* is the actual path to your personal web directory. Your instructor will provide the correct path. Press **Enter** twice.

13. Type **Do While Not guestfile.AtEndOfStream**, and then press **Enter**.

14. Type **First_Name = guestfile.ReadLine**, and then press **Enter**.

15. Type **Last_Name = guestfile.ReadLine**, and then press **Enter**.

16. Type **Gender = guestfile.ReadLine**, and then press **Enter**.

17. Type **Age = guestfile.ReadLine**, and then press **Enter**.

18. Type **Email = guestfile.ReadLine**, and then press **Enter** twice.

19. Type **Response.Write First_Name & "<BR>"**, and then press **Enter**.

20. Type **Response.Write Last_Name & "<BR>"**, and then press **Enter**.

21. Type **Response.Write Gender & "<BR>"**, and then press **Enter**.

22. Type **Response.Write Age & "<BR>"**, and then press **Enter**.

10

23. Type **Response.Write Email & "<P>"**, and then press **Enter**.

24. Type **Loop**, and then press **Enter**.

25. Type **%>**, and then press **Enter**.

26. Type **<H2> The information above has been saved.</H2>**, and then press **Enter**.

27. Type **</BODY>**, and then press **Enter**.

28. Type **</HTML>**, and then press **Enter**.

29. Save the file with the name **showgb.asp** and publish it to your personal web directory. Your completed code should resemble the following:

```
<HTML>
<HEAD>
<TITLE>Guest Book Visitors</TITLE>
</HEAD>
The following people have signed my Guest Book<P>

<% Dim filesys, guestfile, First_Name, Last_Name, Gender,
Age, Email
Set filesys = CreateObject("Scripting.FileSystemObject")
Set guestfile =_
filesys.OpenTextFile( _
    "Server_path_to_your_web_directory\Visitors.txt", 1 )

Do While Not guestfile.AtEndOfStream
First_Name = guestfile.ReadLine
Last_Name = guestfile.ReadLine
Gender = guestfile.ReadLine
Age = guestfile.ReadLine
Email = guestfile.ReadLine

Response.Write First_Name & "<BR>"
Response.Write Last_Name & "<BR>"
Response.Write Gender & "<BR>"
Response.Write Age & "<BR>"
Response.Write Email & "<P>"
Loop
%>
<H2> The information above has been saved.</H2>
</BODY>
</HTML>
```

30. Open Internet Explorer, and then type the URL to your personal web directory.

31. Click the **Guest_Book** link found on the index.html web page.

32. Type the information request by the Guest book page, and then click the **Sign Guest Book** button.

33. Click the **View the Guest Book** link.

34. Verify that all of the information is displayed in the browser window.

35. Close all open windows.

Certification Objectives:

Objectives for the iNet+ Exam:

➤ Understand and be able to describe programming-related terms.

➤ Understand and be able to describe differences between popular client-side and server-side programming languages.

Review Questions

1. Server-side script code is always sent to a client web browser. True or False?

2. A web page can contain both client-side and server-side scripting. True or False?

3. Cookies are stored on the web server and typically contain information about the user and his or her preferences. True or False?

4. An ASP script can be called by typing the URL to the .asp file. True or False?

5. If a web page contains both a client-side and server-side script, which script will be executed first, and why?

_____

_____

_____

_____

_____

6. Describe the difference between a client-side script and a server-side script.

Lab 10.4 XML and Document Type Definitions (DTDs)

Objectives

The objective of this lab is to familiarize you with common terms and provide hands-on experience creating a valid and well-formed XML document. You will also learn to validate an XML document using a Document Type Definition (DTD) file.

To effectively use this lab, you should know the following:

➤ A Document Type Definition (DTD) is a technique used to validate all of the tags, their attributes, and data types in an XML document before it is processed. The validating information can be stored in the XML document or in a separate DTD file.

➤ An XML document is considered to be well-formed only if it obeys the syntax of XML. XML documents that include sequences of markup characters that cannot be parsed or are invalid are not well-formed. An XML document is valid only if it contains a proper document type definition. This means that an XML document can be valid and not well-formed and the reverse is also possible.

➤ The World Wide Web Consortium (W3C) devised the XML standard and the XML specification is available in its entirety at http://www.wc3.org.

➤ An XML parser is an application programming interface (API) designed to read XML code. In addition to parsing XML code, some XML parsers can also validate XML documents using a DTD.

After completing this lab exercise you will be able to:

➤ Create a valid and well-formed XML document

➤ Describe the purpose of a DTD

➤ Validate an XML document using a DTD

➤ Locate more information about XML and the Internet

Materials Required

This lab will require the following:

➤ Windows NT

➤ A lab workgroup size of 2 – 4 students

➤ Microsoft Internet Explorer 5 or later installed on each lab computer

➤ Access to the Internet or the Microsoft XMLint installation zip file

➤ Winzip 7.x or later

Estimated completion time: **1 hour**

ACTIVITY

Do not type the commas or periods as the end of the code that you will type, unless the comma or period is in bold as well.

Download Microsoft Validation Tool:

1. Open Internet Explorer.

2. In the Address bar, type **http://msdn.microsoft.com/downloads/default.asp**, and then press **Enter**.

3. In the left window pane, double-click **Web Development**.

4. Scroll down, if necessary, and double-click **XML**.

5. Scroll down, if necessary, and double-click **XML Validation Tool**.

6. In the right window pane, click **download**.

7. If a license agreement appears, click **Yes**.

8. Click the **Save this file to disk** option button, and then click **OK**.

9. Click **Desktop** in the Save in: list box.

10. Click **Save**.

11. If necessary, click **Close** when the download has completed.

12. Close the browser window.

Install Microsoft Validation Tool:

1. On your desktop, right-click **xmlint.zip**, and then click **Extract to**.

2. In the Extract to: text box, type **C:\XMLint**, and then press **Enter**.

3. Close the Winzip application.

Create an XML document:

1. Click the **Start** button, and then click **Run**.

2. Type **notepad**, and then press **Enter**.

3. In the Notepad window, click **File**, and then click **Save As**.

4. Select **C:** in the Save in: list box.

5. Double-click the **XMLint** yellow folder.

6. In the File name: text box, type **mail.xml**, and then press **Enter**.

7. Type the following XML code into the Notepad window exactly as it appears.

```
<?xml version="1.0" encoding="UTF-8"?>
<!DOCTYPE mail SYSTEM "mail.dtd">
<mail>

<mailbox>

  <mailbox_key>
  <generic_mailbox.first_name>
  CLINT</generic_mailbox.firs  t_name>
  <generic_mailbox.last_name>
  SAXTON</generic_mailbox.last  _name>
  <generic_mailbox.server_location>
  Roseville</generic_mai  lbox.server_location>
  </mailbox_key>
```

```
<generic_mailbox.email_addr>
testaddress@yahoo.com</gene  ric_mailbox.email_addr>

<generic_mailbox.email_addr_alt>
alternate@yahoo.com</generic_mailbox.email_addr_alt>

<generic_mailbox.email_addr_alias>
alternate_test</generic_  mailbox.email_addr_alias>
</mailbox>

</mail>
```

8. In the Notepad window, click **File**, and then click **Save**.

9. Click **File**, and then click **Exit**.

Create a DTD:

1. Click the **Start** button, and then click **Run**.

2. Type **notepad**, and then press **Enter**.

3. In the Notepad window, click **File**, and then click **Save As**.

4. Click **C:** in the Save in: list box.

5. Double-click the **XMLint** yellow folder.

6. In the File name: text box, type **mail.dtd**, and then press **Enter**.

7. Type the following code into the Notepad window exactly as it appears.

```
<!ELEMENT mail (mailbox) >

<!ELEMENT mailbox (mailbox_key,
   generic_mailbox.email_addr,
   generic_mailbox.email_addr_alt,
   generic_mailbox.email_addr_alias) >

<!ELEMENT mailbox_key (generic_mailbox.first_name,
   generic_mailbox.last_name,
   generic_mailbox.server_location) >

<!ELEMENT generic_mailbox.first_name (#PCDATA)>
<!ELEMENT generic_mailbox.last_name (#PCDATA)>

<!ELEMENT generic_mailbox.server_location (#PCDATA)>

<!ELEMENT generic_mailbox.email_addr (#PCDATA) >

<!ELEMENT generic_mailbox.email_addr_alt (#PCDATA) >

<!ELEMENT generic_mailbox.email_addr_alias (#PCDATA) >
```

8. In the Notepad window, click **File**, and then click **Save**.

9. Click **File**, and then click **Exit**.

Validate the XML document:

1. Click the **Start** button, and then click **Run**.

2. Type **command**, and then press **Enter**.

3. In the Command Prompt window, type **cd c:\XMLint**, and then press **Enter**.

4. Type **xmlint.exe mail.xml**, and then press **Enter**.

5. If your XML document contains errors, the appropriate error message will be displayed. Otherwise, the name of the XML file will be displayed.

Certification Objectives:

Objectives for the i–Net+ Exam:

➤ Understand and be able to describe programming-related terms.

➤ Understand and be able to describe differences between popular client-side and server-side programming languages.

➤ Create HTML pages.

➤ Identify the common formats used to deliver content to wireless devices.

10

Review Questions

1. An XML document cannot be validated without a DTD. True or False?

2. A well-formed XML document must have a DTD. True or False?

3. To be considered well-formed, both an XML document and its DTD must contain the <?xml version="1.0" encoding="UTF=8"?> processing instruction at the beginning of their respective files. True or False?

4. A DTD can be either a separate file or appear in the same file as the XML document. True or False?

5. An XML document cannot be both valid and well-formed. True or False?

6. On the lines provided, describe the difference between a valid XML document and a well-formed XML document.

_____

_____

_____

_____

_____

DATABASES AND WEB HOSTING

Labs included in this chapter

➤ Lab 11.1 Creating a Microsoft Access Database

➤ Lab 11.2 Reading from a Database Using ASP

➤ Lab 11.3 Writing to a Database Using ASP

i-Net+ Exam Objectives	
Objective	**Lab**
Understand and be able to describe programming-related terms.	11.1, 11.2, 11.3
Understand when to use popular tools to connect a Web server to a database.	11.1, 11.2, 11.3

LAB 11.1 CREATING A MICROSOFT ACCESS DATABASE

Objectives

The objective of this lab is to familiarize you with how databases are utilized and some of the more common terminology associated with databases. During this lab, you will create a database using Microsoft Access 2000. In Labs 11.2 and 11.3, you will use the database you create in this lab to read and write data to and from a web page.

To effectively work through this lab, you should know the following:

➤ A relational database management system (RDBMS) is software that controls a relational database. Commands received by the RDBMS manage database activity such as adding, deleting, updating, sorting, and selecting records. In addition to these commands, the RDBMS is responsible for maintaining the integrity of the relational database structure.

➤ A primary key is a field, or fields, used to define the entries that make a single row unique within a table. No two rows within a table can have the same primary key.

➤ A relational database holds data in a group of tables that can be related to one another by columns they have in common. Most databases today are relational.

➤ A hierarchical database uses a top-down design with major categories at the top and less significant categories at the bottom.

➤ In a relational database, a field is also known as a column.

➤ A data warehouse is a repository of data that has been collected into one or more databases, but is no longer actively needed for processing.

➤ Data mining is the study of data in a data warehouse, with the intention of discovering information useful to predict future direction for a company.

➤ Data mart is a portion of data in a data warehouse that is identified as useful to a certain target group of data miners.

➤ A distributed database is a database stored on more than one computer. Portions of the database can be presented to a user in such a way that the user is unaware that the data is coming from more than one computer.

➤ A database administrator is the person responsible for the overall integrity of the data in a database and the security of the database.

After completing this lab, you will be able to:

➤ Define the term relational database

➤ Define the term relational database management system (RDBMS)

➤ Create a database using Microsoft Access 2000

➤ Create a table and add data to a Microsoft Access database

Materials Required

This lab will require the following:

➤ Windows 9x

➤ A lab workgroup size of 2–4 students

➤ Internet Explorer 5.0 or later

➤ Microsoft Access 2000 installed on each lab computer

➤ Students must be able to map a network drive to their assigned share on the web server and be provided the UNC path to connect. Student must also be provided the URL to view their personal web directory.

Estimated completion time: **45 minutes**

ACTIVITY

Create a Microsoft Access database:

1. Click **Start**, point to **Programs**, and then click **Microsoft Access**. If prompted by a dialog box, click **Cancel**.

2. Click **File**, and then click **New**.

3. Double-click **Database**.

4. Click the **Save in:** drop-down list arrow, and then click **Desktop**.

5. In the File name: text box, type **MyDatabase**.

6. Click **Create**.

Create a table:

Do not type the commas or periods at the end of code that you will type, unless the comma or period is in bold as well.

1. Double-click **Create table by using wizard**.

2. Click **FirstName**, and then click the **>** button.

3. Click **LastName**, and then click the **>** button.

4. Click **Address**, and then click the **>** button.

5. Click **City**, and then click the **>** button.

6. Click **State,** and then click the **>** button.

7. Click **PostalCode**, and then click the **>** button.

8. Click **HomePhone**, and then click the **>** button.

11

9. Click **Next**.

10. Type **Student_Database**.

11. Click the **Yes, set a primary key for me.** option button, if necessary.

12. Click **Next**.

13. Click **Finish**.

Add data to the table:

1. In the First Name text box, type your first name.

2. In the Last Name text box, type your last name.

3. In the Address text box, type a fictitious address.

4. In the City text box, type a city name.

5. In the State text box, type a state name.

6. In the Postal Code text box, type a fictitious postal code.

7. In the Home Phone text box, type a fictitious phone number.

8. Repeat Steps 1–7 until every student in the lab workgroup has an entry in the database.

Certification Objectives:

Objectives for the i-Net+ Exam:

➤ Understand and be able to describe programming-related terms.

➤ Understand when to use popular tools to connect a Web server to a database.

Review Questions

1. A relational database management system is responsible for receiving and executing commands from users and maintaining database integrity. True or False?

2. A hierarchical database stores data in tables that can be related to each other. True or False?

3. Data stored in a data warehouse is typically archived data and is no longer used by the systems that produced the data. True or False?

4. Two different databases sending commands to each other is an example of a distributed database. True or False?

5. A DBA is the person ultimately responsible for the integrity and management of a database. True or False?

6. In the database you created in this lab, what is the field name of the primary key?

_____

_____

_____

_____

_____

LAB 11.2 READING FROM A DATABASE USING ASP

Objectives

The objective of this lab is to familiarize you with the methods used to read data from a database. During this lab exercise, you will develop a Web page named index.html and use the Web page to read data from the database you created in Lab 11.1.

The following list gives you database terminology that will help you understand the lab activity:

➤ A Data Source Name (DSN) is a method used to reference a database. A DSN describes important information about a database such as the path and driver used to access it.

➤ Open Database Connectivity (ODBC) provides a connection between an application and a database on a network.

➤ Java Database Connectivity (JDBC) is a technology similar to ODBC that provides an interface between a Java program and a database.

➤ In relational databases, a record is one row within one table of the database.

➤ A recordset is a group of records in a database currently available to a program to be written to or read from.

➤ ADO includes many interrelated objects that have different functions and properties. To programmatically use an ADO function or property, you must include either the adovbs.inc file, or for Java, the adojavas.inc file.

➤ ADODB (ActiveX Data Object Database) provides a standard set of commands to communicate between a program and a database. In this lab, you will include the adovbs.inc file in your script because you will be using ADODB functions to connect to your database.

➤ The Structured Query Language (SQL) is a set of commands and arguments used to manage a database. It is universally accepted as the defacto standard by the industry. Most relational databases accept SQL commands.

➤ A query is a request for data from a database that can be used for an on-screen display or in a printed report. Most database queries are done using SQL.

11

After completing this lab exercise, you will be able to:

➤ Define the term DSN and describe its relationship to ODBC.

➤ Create an ASP web page that can retrieve data from a database.

➤ Write data from a recordset in HTML format to be displayed on a web page.

Materials Required

This lab will require the following:

➤ Windows 9x

➤ A lab workgroup size of 2–4 students

➤ Microsoft Internet Explorer 5 or later installed on each lab computer

➤ An IIS 4.0 Windows NT web server configured to execute ASP scripts

➤ Completion of Lab 11.1

➤ Students must be able to map a network drive to their assigned share on the web server and be provided the UNC path to connect. Students must also be provided the URL to view their personal web directory.

➤ The instructor must share a folder that holds the adovbs.inc file so that the workgroup can publish the file to their personal web directory.

➤ Each lab workgroup must choose one database to use for their group, publish the database to their personal directory, and then request a DSN from the instructor. After the instructor has created a DSN for the group's database, begin the activity.

Estimated completion time: **1 hour**

ACTIVITY

Publish adovbs.inc:

1. Right-click **Network Neighborhood** on your desktop, and then click **Map Network Drive**.

2. In the Path: text box, type the UNC path provided by your instructor, and then click **OK**.

3. Click and drag the **adovbs.inc** file to your desktop.

4. Close the window that contains the adovbs.inc file.

5. Right-click **Network Neighborhood**, and then click **Disconnect Network Drive**.

6. In the Disconnect Network Drive window, double-click the drive letter that is associated with the UNC path you typed in Step 1.

7. Publish **adovbs.inc** to your personal web directory.

Create and Publish index.html:

1. Click **Start**, and then click **Run**.

2. Type **Notepad**, and then press **Enter**.

3. Type **<HTML>**, and then press **Enter**.

4. Type **<H1>My Database Page</H1>**, and then press **Enter**.

5. Type **<A HREF="read_data.asp">Student_Database</A>**, and then press **Enter**.

6. Type **</HTML>**, and then press **Enter**.

7. Click **File**, click **Save**, and then save the file as **index.html** on your desktop.

8. Publish **index.html** to your personal web directory.

Connect to the database and Create the "InDatabase" recordset:

1. Click **Start**, and then click **Run**.

2. Type **Notepad**, and then press **Enter**.

3. Type **<HTML>**, and then press **Enter**.

4. Type **<BODY>**, and then press **Enter**.

5. Type **<H1>Student Database</H1>**, and then press **Enter** twice.

6. Type **<!— #INCLUDE FILE="adovbs.inc" —>**, and then press **Enter**.

7. Type **<%**, and then press **Enter**.

8. Type **Dim Connect, InDatabase**, and then press **Enter**. (You will type the first comma, but not the second.)

9. Type

   Set Connect = Server.CreateObject("ADODB.Connection"), and then press **Enter**.

10. Type **Connect.Open "*yourDSNhere*"**, where *yourDSNhere* is the DSN provided by your instructor, and then press **Enter**. Warning: You may need to specify a default driver if you are using a Windows 2000 web server or a later version of IIS. To specify a default driver, type **Connect.Open "Driver={Microsoft Access Driver (*.mdb)}; DBQ=*yourDSNhere*"**, and then press **Enter**.

11. Type **Set InDatabase = Connect.Execute(_**, and then press **Enter**.

12. Type **"SELECT * FROM Student_Database ORDER BY Student_DatabaseID")**, and then press **Enter**. The code that you just typed is the SQL command that you are sending to the database. The command reads all records from your database and returns them in numerical order by Student_DatabaseID.

13. Type **do until InDatabase.EOF**, and then press **Enter**.

14. Type **%>** to end the script.

15. Click **File**, and then click **Save**. Save the file to your desktop with the name **read_data.asp** and publish it to your personal web directory. Your completed file should resemble the following:

```
<HTML>
<BODY>
<H1>Student Database</H1>
<!-- #INCLUDE FILE="adovbs.inc" -->
<%
Dim Connect, InDatabase
Set Connect = Server.CreateObject("ADODB.Connection")
Connect.Open "STUDENT"
Set InDatabase = Connect.Execute( _
"SELECT * FROM Student_Database BY Student_DatabaseID")
do until InDatabase.EOF
%>
```

Write the "InDatabase" recordset in HTML format:

Throughout this lab, the fields in the steps must match the column names in the database you created in Lab 11.1.

1. Open the read_data.asp file in Notepad if it is not already open. Place the answer at the end of the file.

2. Type **StudentDatabaseID:<%=InDatabase("Student_DatabaseID")%>
, and then press **Enter.

3. Type **Name: <%=InDatabase("FirstName")%>**, and then press **Enter**.

4. Type **<%=InDatabase("LastName")%>
, and then press **Enter.

5. Type **Street Addr: <%=InDatabase("Address")%>
, and then press **Enter.

6. Type **City: <%=InDatabase("City")%>
, and then press **Enter.

7. Type **State: <%=InDatabase("State")%>
, and then press **Enter.

8. Type **Zip: <%=InDatabase("PostalCode")%>
, and then press **Enter.

9. Type **Home Phone: <%=InDatabase("HomePhone")%>
, and then press **Enter.

10. Type **<% InDatabase.MoveNext %>**, and then press **Enter**.

11. Type **<% loop %>**, and then press **Enter**.

12. Type **</BODY>**, and then press **Enter**.

13. Type **</HTML>**, and then press **Enter**.

14. Save the file with the name **read_data.asp** and publish it to your personal web directory. Your complete read_data.asp page should resemble the following:

```
<HTML>
<BODY>
<H1>Student Database</H1>

<!- #INCLUDE FILE="adovbs.inc" ->
<%
Dim Connect, InDatabase
Set Connect = Server.CreateObject("ADODB.Connection")
Connect.Open "STUDENT"
Set InDatabase = Connect.Execute( _
"SELECT * FROM Student_Database ORDER BY Student_Database
ID")
do until InDatabase.EOF
%>


StudentDatabaseID:
<%=InDatabase("Student_DatabaseID")%><BR>
Name:
<%=InDatabase("FirstName")%>
<%=InDatabase("LastName")%><BR>
Street Addr:
<%=InDatabase("Address")%><BR>
City:
<%=InDatabase("City")%><BR>
State:
<%=InDatabase("State")%><BR>
Zip:
<%=InDatabase("PostalCode")%><BR>
Home Phone:
<%=InDatabase("HomePhone")%><BR>
<% InDatabase.MoveNext loop %>
</BODY>
</HTML>
```

15. Close Notepad.

16. Open Internet Explorer, and then type the URL to your personal web directory.

17. Click the **Student_Database** link on the index.html web page.

18. Verify that the information displayed by read_data.asp is the same information found in your database. Then try adding data to the database and refreshing the read_data.asp web page.

11

Certification Objectives:

Objectives for the i-Net+ Exam:

➤ Understand and be able to describe programming-related terms.

➤ Understand when to use popular tools to connect a Web server to a database.

Review Questions

1. ODBC and JDBC provide connectivity between a database and an application. True or False?

2. A DSN must be configured on the client computer before a web page can access a database. True or False?

3. Describe the relationship between a record and recordset.

_____

_____

_____

_____

_____

4. In your own words, describe how the read_data.asp web page used a recordset to read data from your database.

_____

_____

_____

_____

_____

5. Describe the difference between a record and a field in a relational database.

_____

_____

_____

_____

_____

6. Describe three ways you can envision web/database interaction being used in the workplace.

_____

_____

_____

_____

_____

LAB 11.3 WRITING TO A DATABASE USING ASP

Objectives

The objective of this lab is to familiarize you with the methods used to write data to a database. During this lab exercise you will use an HTML form to write data to the database you created in Lab 11.1. The HTML form you create will post data to an ASP web page that will use an ADODB connection to write to the database, similarly to how you read data from your database in Lab 11.2.

After completing this lab, you will be able to:

➤ Create an HTML form and post data to an ASP Web page

➤ Create an ASP Web page that will write records to a database

Materials Required

This lab will require the following:

➤ Windows 9x

➤ A lab workgroup size of 2–4 students

➤ Completion of Lab 11.1 and Lab 11.2

➤ Microsoft Internet Explorer 5 or later installed on each lab computer

➤ A web server configured to execute ASP scripts

➤ Students must be able to map a network drive to their assigned share on the web server and be provided the UNC path to connect. Students must also be provided the URL to view their personal web directory.

➤ The instructor must share a folder that contains the adovbs.inc file so that the workgroup can publish the file to their personal web directory.

➤ Each lab workgroup must choose one database to use for their group, publish the database to their personal directory, and then request a DSN from the instructor. After the instructor has created a DSN for the group's database, begin the activity.

> Estimated completion time: **1 hour**

ACTIVITY

Create form.html:

1. Click **Start**, and then click **Run**.

2. Type **Notepad**, and then click **OK**.

3. Type **<HTML>**, and then press **Enter**.

4. Type **<HEAD>**, and then press **Enter**.

5. Type **<TITLE> Add to Student Database</TITLE>**, and then press **Enter**.

6. Type **</HEAD>**, and then press **Enter**.

7. Type **<BODY>**, and then press **Enter**.

8. Type **<H1>Add to Student Database</H1>**, and then press **Enter** twice.

9. Type **<FORM METHOD="POST" ACTION="write_data.asp">**, and then press **Enter**.

10. Type **First name: <INPUT TYPE="text" SIZE="20" NAME="First_Name"><P>**, and then press **Enter**.

11. Type **Last name: <INPUT TYPE="text" SIZE="20" NAME="Last_Name"><P>**, and then press **Enter**.

12. Type **Address: <INPUT TYPE="text" SIZE="20" NAME="Address"><P>**, and then press **Enter**.

13. Type **City: <INPUT TYPE="text" SIZE="20" NAME="City"><P>**, and then press **Enter**.

14. Type **State: <INPUT TYPE="text" SIZE="20" NAME="State"><P>**, and then press **Enter**.

15. Type **Zip_Code: <INPUT TYPE="text" SIZE="20" NAME="Zip_Code"><P>**, and then press **Enter**.

16. Type **Home_Phone: <INPUT TYPE="text" SIZE="20" NAME="Home_Phone"><P>**, and then press **Enter**.

17. Type **<INPUT TYPE="submit" VALUE="Add" ><P>**, and then press **Enter**.

18. Type **</FORM>**, and then press **Enter**.

19. Type **</BODY>**, and then press **Enter**.

20. Type **</HTML>**, and then press **Enter**.

21. Save the file as **form.html** and publish it to your personal web directory. The complete form.html Web page should resemble the following:

```
<HTML>
<HEAD>
<TITLE>Add to Student Database</TITLE>
</HEAD>
<BODY>
<H1>Add to Student Database</H1>

<FORM METHOD="POST" ACTION="write_data.asp">
First name:
<INPUT TYPE="text" SIZE="20" NAME="First_Name"><P>
Last name:
<INPUT TYPE="text" SIZE="20" NAME="Last_Name"><P>
Address:
<INPUT TYPE="text" SIZE="20" NAME="Address"><P>
City:
<INPUT TYPE="text" SIZE="20" NAME="City"><P>
State:
<INPUT TYPE="text" SIZE="20" NAME="State"><P>
Zip_Code:
<INPUT TYPE="text" SIZE="20" NAME="Zip_Code"><P>
Home_Phone:
<INPUT TYPE="text" SIZE="20" NAME="Home_Phone"><P>
<INPUT TYPE="submit" VALUE="Add" ><P>
</FORM>
</BODY>
</HTML>
```

Edit the index.html:

1. Connect to your personal web directory.

2. Using Notepad edit the index.html file you create in Lab 11.2.

3. Move your cursor to the end of the line containing the "Student_Database" hyperlink, and then press **Enter**.

4. Type **<A HREF="form.html">Add_to_Student_Database</A>**, and then press **Enter**.

5. Save the file and close Notepad.

Connecting to the database and opening a new recordset:

1. Click **Start**, and then click **Run**.

2. Type **Notepad**, and then press **Enter**.

3. Type **<HTML>**, and then press **Enter**.

4. Type **<BODY>**, and then press **Enter**.

5. Type **<TITLE>database update </TITLE>**, and then press **Enter** twice.

6. Type **<!— #INCLUDE FILE="adovbs.inc" —>**, and then press **Enter**.

7. Type **<%**, and then press **Enter**.

8. Type **Dim Connect, ObjRecordset**, and then press **Enter**. (You will type the first period, but not the second.)

9. Type **Set Connect = Server.CreateObject("ADODB.Connection")**, and then press **Enter**.

10. Type **Connect.Open "*yourDSNhere*"**, where *yourDSNhere* is the DSN provided by your instructor. Press **Enter**. Warning: You may need to specify a default driver if you are using a Windows 2000 web server or a later version of IIS. To specify a default driver, type
**Connect.open "Driver={Microsoft Access Driver (*.mdb)};
DBQ=*yourDSNhere*"**, and then press **Enter**.

11. Type **Set ObjRecordset = Server.CreateObject("ADODB.Recordset")**, and then press **Enter**.

12. Type

    ObjRecordset.Open "Student_Database", Connect, adOpenKeyset, adLockOptimistic, adCmdTable, and then press **Enter**. (Do not type the comma that comes before "and".)

13. Type **ObjRecordset.AddNew**, and then press **Enter** twice.

Adding data to the recordset and updating the database:

1. Type **ObjRecordset("FirstName") = Request.Form("First_Name")**, and then press **Enter**.

2. Type **ObjRecordset("LastName") = Request.Form("Last_Name")**, and then press **Enter**.

3. Type

ObjRecordset("Address") = Request.Form("Address"), and then press **Enter**.

4. Type

ObjRecordset("City") = Request.Form("City"), and then press **Enter**.

5. Type

ObjRecordset("State") = Request.Form("State"), and then press **Enter**.

6. Type

ObjRecordset("PostalCode") = Request.Form("Zip_Code"), and then press **Enter**.

7. Type

ObjRecordset("HomePhone") = Request.Form("Home_Phone"), and then press **Enter**.

8. Type **ObjRecordset.Update**, and then press **Enter**.

9. Type **%>** to end the script and press **Enter** twice.

10. Type **<FONT SIZE="5">The Database has been updated! </FONT>
, and then press **Enter.

11. Type **</BODY>**, and then press **Enter**.

12. Type **</HTML>**, and then press **Enter**.

13. Save the file as **write_data.asp** and publish it to your personal web directory. Your complete write_data.asp Web page should resemble the following:

```
<HTML>
<BODY>
<TITLE>database update </TITLE>

<!--#INCLUDE FILE="adovbs.inc" -->

<%
Dim Connect, ObjRecordset
Set Connect = Server.CreateObject("ADODB.Connection")
Connect.Open "STUDENT"
Set ObjRecordset = Server.CreateObject("ADODB.Recordset")
ObjRecordset.Open "Student_Database", Connect,
adOpenKeyset, adLockOptimistic, adCmdTable
  ObjRecordset.AddNew
  ObjRecordset("First Name") = Request.Form("First_Name")
  ObjRecordset("Last Name") = Request.Form("Last_Name")
  ObjRecordset("Address") = Request.Form("Address")
  ObjRecordset("City") = Request.Form("City")
  ObjRecordset("State") = Request.Form("State")
  ObjRecordset("Postal Code") = Request.Form("Zip_Code")
  ObjRecordset("Home Phone") = Request.Form("Home_Phone")
  ObjRecordset.Update
%>

<FONT SIZE="5">The Database has been
  updated!</FONT><BR>
</BODY>
</HTML>
```

14. Close Notepad.

15. Open Internet Explorer, and then type the URL to your personal web directory.

16. Click the **Add to Student Database** link on the index.html web page.

17. Verify that all of the information you entered on form.html was added to your database.

11

Certification Objectives:

Objectives for the i-Net+ Exam:

➤ Understand and be able to describe programming-related terms.

➤ Understand when to use popular tools to connect a Web server to a database.

Review Questions

1. When using ASP, you must create a recordset before adding data to a database. True or False?

2. A recordset can contain more than one record. True or False?

3. In the previous activity, the "ObjRecordset.AddNew" instruction created a new recordset to be added to the database. True or False?

4. In the previous activity, the ASP page is also the confirmation page. True or False?

5. The Request.Data("variable") is the instruction used to retrieve data from an HTML form. True or False?

6. A form variable name cannot be different than the database field name where it will be loaded. True or False?

12 INTERNET SECURITY

Labs included in this chapter

➤ Lab 12.1 Security Research Project

➤ Lab 12.2 Using PGP (Pretty Good Privacy) Encryption

➤ Lab 12.3 Virus Protection

---

i-Net+ Exam Objectives

Objective	Lab
Understand and be able to describe various Internet security concepts.	12.1
Identify appropriate access-control security features for an Internet server.	12.1
Describe how firewalls are used to protect private networks.	12.1
Identify when to use various DMZ configurations.	12.1
Understand and be able to describe various authentication/encryption technologies.	12.1, 12.2
Be able to describe the uses of various client security add-ons and when to use them.	12.2
Be able to describe the use of anti-virus software and when to use it.	12.3

LAB 12.1 SECURITY RESEARCH PROJECT

Objectives

The objective of this lab is to provide you with an overview of the many network security technologies available.

You must protect your network against hackers. A hacker is anyone who attempts to gain access to a network or computer with malicious intent. There are many different types of network attacks that have been used by hackers, including the following:

➤ A Denial of Service (DoS) attack is a method used to flood a host with requests until it can no longer respond. A ping flood is a type of DoS attack that happens when a host is flooded with ping requests to the point that the server cannot function. It is also known as ICMP flooding.

➤ A ping of death is a type of DoS attack that happens when a ping is sent with a packet larger than the standard 64 bytes. This packet size causes the system that received the ping request to shut down.

➤ SYN flooding is a flooding attack that uses the synchronization feature of TCP to cause a server to shut down.

After completing this lab, you will be able to:

➤ Define and describe the use of Public Key Infrastructure (PKI)

➤ Define and describe the use of a virtual private network (VPN)

➤ Define and describe the use of the Secure Sockets Layer (SSL) protocol, digital certificates, digital signatures, access control lists (ACLs), and smart cards

➤ Define and describe the use of Internet Protocol Security (IPSec), firewalls, and demilitarized zones (DMZs)

Materials Required

This lab will require the following:

➤ Windows 9x

➤ A lab workgroup size of 2–4 students

➤ Microsoft Internet Explorer 5 or later

Estimated completion time: **1 hour**

ACTIVITY

Security research:

For each of the following technologies, use the Internet or other resources to define the technology. Then, describe a scenario in which this technology is utilized in business. One excellent resource for this activity is *www.whatis.com*.

1. Public Key Infrastructure (PKI)

   Definition:

   _____

   _____

   _____

   _____

   _____

   Scenario:

   _____

   _____

   _____

   _____

   _____

2. Virtual private network (VPN)

   Definition:

   _____

   _____

   _____

   _____

   Scenario:

   _____

   _____

   _____

   _____

   _____

12

3. Secure Sockets Layer (SSL)

Definition:

_____

_____

_____

_____

_____

Scenario:

_____

_____

_____

_____

_____

4. Digital certificates

Definition:

_____

_____

_____

_____

_____

Scenario:

_____

_____

_____

_____

5. Digital signatures

Definition:

_____

_____

_____

_____

Scenario:

_____

_____

_____

_____

_____

6. Access control lists (ACLs)

Definition:

_____

_____

_____

_____

_____

Scenario:

_____

_____

_____

_____

_____

7. Smart cards

Definition:

_____

_____

_____

_____

_____

Scenario:

_____

_____

_____

_____

_____

12

8. Internet Protocol Security (IPSec)

Definition:

_____

_____

_____

_____

_____

Scenario:

_____

_____

_____

_____

_____

9. Firewalls

Definition:

_____

_____

_____

_____

_____

Scenario:

_____

_____

_____

_____

_____

10. DMZs, such as bastion hosts, three-homed firewalls, and back-to-back firewalls

Definition:

_____

_____

_____

_____

_____

Scenario:

_____

_____

_____

_____

_____

Certification Objectives

Objectives for the i-Net+ Exam:

➤ Understand and be able to describe various Internet security concepts.

➤ Identify appropriate access-control security features for an Internet server.

➤ Describe how firewalls are used to protect private networks.

➤ Identify when to use various DMZ configurations.

➤ Understand and be able to describe various authentication/encryption technologies.

Review Questions

1. Web servers use VPN connections to process secure credit card transactions. True or False?

2. A ping command can create an ICMP flood. True or False?

3. The "ping of death" is an example of a DoS attack. True or False?

4. A smart card is a new technology for credit card transactions. True or False?

5. An ACL can be implemented on a router. True or False?

6. From home, Joan has a DSL connection to the Internet. Her company has recently added a new service that allows employees like Joan to connect to the company's intranet using a VPN connection. Joan would like to telecommute. Can the new VPN service benefit Joan? If so, describe how she could connect to her employer's intranet.

_____

_____

_____

_____

_____

12

LAB 12.2 USING PGP (PRETTY GOOD PRIVACY) ENCRYPTION

Objectives

The objective of this lab is to provide you with hands-on experience using PGP encryption.

Encryption is the process of coding data to prevent unauthorized parties from viewing or changing it. Pretty Good Privacy encryption (PGP) is a popular encryption system that uses three keys: a private key, a public key, and a short key that is generated by the encryption software. Figure 12-1 illustrates how the PGP software utilizes all three keys.

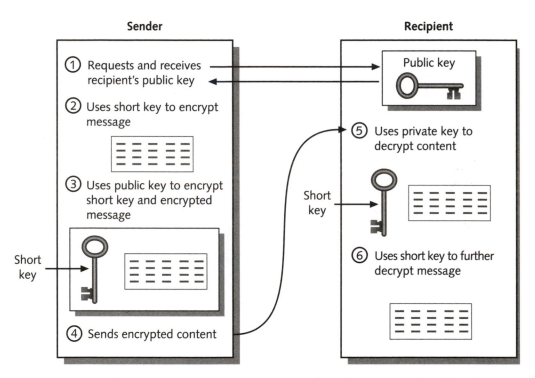

Sender

1. Requests and receives recipient's public key
2. Uses short key to encrypt message
3. Uses public key to encrypt short key and encrypted message

Short key

4. Sends encrypted content

Recipient

Public key

5. Uses private key to decrypt content

Short key

6. Uses short key to further decrypt message

Figure 12-1   With Pretty Good Privacy Encryption, three keys are used: a short key and the recipient's public and private keys

As shown in Figure 12-1, PGP utilizes a public and private key system. The public key is used for encrypting messages, and the private key is used with a public key to encrypt/decrypt messages. For example, an encrypted message can be sent by using the sender's private key and the recipient's public key to encrypt the message. In this way, only the recipient's private key and public key combination will be able to decrypt the message.

After completing this lab, you will be able to:

➤ Install software that implements PGP encryption

➤ Create a private key

➤ Encrypt a file using PGP

➤ Decrypt a file using PGP

Materials Required

This lab will require the following:

➤ Windows 9x

➤ A lab workgroup size of 2–4 students

➤ Microsoft Internet Explorer 5 or later

➤ To complete this lab activity, you must download or have previously down-loaded PGP Freeware from *www.pgp.com*.

Estimated completion time: **45 minutes**

ACTIVITY

Installing PGP freeware:

The following steps are for the installation of PGP Freeware version 7.0.3. For different versions of PGP software, the exact steps may vary.

12

1. Double-click the **PGPFreeware 7.0.3.exe** installation file to begin the installation.

2. Click **Next**.

3. Click **Yes** to agree to the license agreement.

4. Click **Next**.

5. Click **No I am a New User**, and then click **Next**.

6. Click **Next**.

7. Click **Next**.

8. Click **Next**.

9. Click **Next**; the files will be copied to your hard drive.

10. Click **Select All**, and then click **OK**.

11. Click **Finish** and your computer will restart.

Creating a PGP key:

 If the Key Generation Wizard doesn't automatically open after restarting your computer at the end of Step 11 in the previous set of steps, begin at Step 1 in this series of steps. Otherwise, begin at Step 4.

1. Click **Start**, point to **Programs**, and then point to **PGP**.
2. Click **PGPkeys**.
3. In the PGPkeys window, click the **Keys** menu, and then click **New Key**.
4. Click **Next** in the Key Generation Wizard window.
5. Type your name and email address, and then click **Next**.
6. Enter a pass phrase. A pass phrase is similar to a password.
7. In the Confirm pass phrase: text box, retype the pass phrase you typed in Step 6. Click **Nex**t.
8. Click **Next**.
9. Click **Finish**.
10. Click **File** on the menu bar, and then click **Exit**.

Encrypt a file:

1. Click **Start**.
2. Point to **Programs**, point to **PGP**, and then click **PGPtools**.
3. On the PGPtool bar, click the **Encrypt** button, which appears as an envelope with a closed lock. It is the second button from the left.
4. Select a file to encrypt, and then click **Open**.
5. Click **OK** and the file will be encrypted and placed in the same directory as the source file. The encrypted file will have a .pgp extension.

Decrypt a file:

1. Double-click the file that you encrypted.
2. Enter your pass phrase in the Pass phrase: text box, and then click **OK**.
3. The file will be decrypted and you will be prompted to save the file. Navigate to the folder where you want to store the file, and then click **Save**.

Certification Objectives

Objectives for the i–Net+ Exam:

➤ Be able to describe the uses of various client security add–ons and when to use them.

➤ Understand and be able to describe various authentication/encryption technologies.

Review Questions

1. A recipient's public key is required to send them a PGP encrypted message. True or False?

2. To use a private key, you must provide a pass phrase. True or False?

3. Encrypted data can only be viewed in Notepad. True or False?

4. PGP can be used to encrypt files and e-mail messages. True or False?

5. Only a public key is required to encrypt messages. True or False?

6. If you lose your private key, you can create a new private key and decrypt a message that was encrypted using your old public key. True or False?

LAB 12.3 VIRUS PROTECTION

12

Objectives

A virus is a program designed with malicious intent. Viruses can damage your computer by deleting and corrupting data. The objective of this lab is to familiarize you with installing and using antivirus software.

All viruses are programs written by programmers. Your computer can contract a virus through many different forms of communication, such as disks, file downloads, e-mail, and even web sites.

A virus definition file is program file. It is used by antivirus software to recognize patterns of known viruses. When a new virus is identified, the software vendor will normally release a new virus definition file to their customers. To be protected against all the latest viruses, you must regularly update your virus definition file.

Programmers write viruses to cause damage. The damage that a virus is designed to cause is the virus payload. Some viruses may only draw a strange figure on your screen; others may attempt to delete files from your hard drive.

After completing this lab, you will be able to:

➤ Install Norton Antivirus (home user version)

➤ Use Norton to scan your hard drive for viruses

Materials Required

This lab will require the following:

➤ Windows 9x

➤ A lab workgroup size of 2–4 students

➤ Microsoft Outlook Express 5 or later

➤ To complete this lab you must either download the Norton Antivirus Windows 95/98/Me evaluation copy or own a licensed version of the software. If you are going to download the Norton evaluation software, you must have an Internet connection.

Estimated completion time: **45 minutes**

ACTIVITY

Installing the software:

 These steps follow the installation of Norton Antivirus Windows 95/98/ME. For different versions of the software, the exact steps may vary.

1. Click the **Launch** button after the download has completed. This will start the installation program.

2. Click **Next**.

3. Click **Yes**.

4. Click **Next**.

5. Click **Next**.

6. Click **Next**.

7. On the registration screen, click **Next**.

8. Uncheck all check boxes, and then click **Next**.

9. Enter your contact information, and then click **Next**.

10. Enter your address information, and then click **Next**.

11. Answer all seven questions, and then click **Next**.

12. Click **Next**.

13. Click **Finish**.

14. Continue the product installation by clicking **Next**.

15. Click **Next**.

16. Click **Next**.

17. Click **Next**.

18. On the Live Update screen, click **Next**.

19. Click **Next**.

20. Click **Finish**. Your computer reboots.

21. Norton will start to scan your file system. Click **Stop** to terminate the scan, and then click **Close** in the Scan Results dialog box.

Scanning for viruses:

1. Click **Start**, point to **Programs**, point to **Norton Antivirus**, and then click **Norton AntiVirus 2001**.

2. Click **Scan for Viruses**.

3. Click **Run Scan Now** to begin scanning for viruses on your computer.

4. When Norton AntiVirus has finished the scan, read the Scan Results dialog box and take the appropriate action(s).

5. Close the Norton application when you have finished.

Researching viruses and describing their symptoms:

Use the Internet and other research materials available to you to identify five viruses that belong to each of the following virus categories.

1. Boot sector viruses

_____

_____

_____

_____

_____

12

2. Worms

_____

_____

_____

_____

_____

_____

3. Trojan horses

_____

_____

_____

_____

_____

4. Macro viruses

_____

_____

_____

_____

_____

5. Multipartite viruses

_____

_____

_____

_____

_____

6. Stealth viruses

_____

_____

_____

_____

_____

7. Partition table viruses

_____

_____

_____

_____

_____

8. Virus hoaxes

_____

_____

_____

_____

_____

Certification Objectives

Objectives for the i-Net+ Exam:

➤ Be able to describe the use of anti-virus software and when to use it.

Review Questions

1. A virus is really a type of application defect and can often be resolved by installing a service pack or application update. True or False?

2. Updating your virus definition file regularly will help your antivirus software protect you from the latest computer viruses. True or False?

3. A virus can cause fatal damage to your operating system. True or False?

4. The intended action of a virus is called the virus's payload. True or False?

5. What are two things that you can do to help prevent the spread of viruses?

_____

_____

_____

_____

12

6. Name three ways that a computer virus can be contracted.

_____

_____

_____

_____

_____

CHAPTER THIRTEEN

DOING BUSINESS ON THE WEB

Labs included in this chapter

➤ Lab 13.1 Understanding Business on the Web

➤ Lab 13.2 E-Commerce and Transaction Processing

➤ Lab 13.3 Copyrights and Trademarks

---

i-Net+ Exam Objectives	
Objective	**Lab**
Recognize and explain the most up-to-date types of e-business models being applied today.	13.1
Identify key factors relating to strategic marketing considerations as they relate to launching an e-business initiative.	13.1
Understand and be able to describe e-commerce terms and concepts.	13.2
Identify key factors relating to legal and regulatory considerations when planning e-business solutions.	13.3

LAB 13.1 UNDERSTANDING BUSINESS ON THE WEB

Objectives

The objective of this lab is to provide you with an understanding of the many different types of e-business and e-business models that can be found on the Internet today.

When most people think of online businesses, they immediately think of companies that sell products over the Internet. These types of companies generally fall into the following two categories:

➤ E-tailers sell products over the Internet and only over the Internet.

➤ Brick-and-click companies establish a web presence to supplement existing retail businesses. One example of a popular brick-and-click is *www.barnesandnoble.com*.

Although e-tailing and brick-and-click businesses are successful on the Web, they are not alone. Other business types include the following:

➤ Online service businesses provide a service over the Internet. They include job placement, resume writing, loan processing, gambling, and other services.

➤ A downloadable file business sells a product that can be downloaded immediately after the customer has paid for the product. Some examples of downloadable file businesses include music, software, and blueprint sales.

➤ An auction business hosts a web site that conducts online auctions. One example of a popular online auction business is *www.ebay.com*.

➤ An ASP (application service provider) is a company that stores application software on its web site and then allows customers to use the software via the Internet for a fee.

As you can see, there are numerous types of e-businesses on the Internet. Likewise, there are almost as many different e-business models utilized by various companies on the Internet. Some of the more common e-business models include the following:

➤ A business-to-business (B2C) web site is designed to manually (point-and-click) and automatically sell products and services to other businesses.

➤ A business-to-consumer (B2C) web site is designed to sell products and services to consumers. B2C web sites often provide shopping cart interfaces for their customers and have the ability to upsell other products based on a customer's preferences.

➤ Business-to-employee (B2E) web sites are designed to improve business communication by providing information about personnel listings, job postings, and human resources. In some cases, a company may create a B2E web site to sell its products at a discounted rate to employees.

➤ A business-to-government web site is designed sell products or services to government agencies. Many companies exist today that only provide products or services to governments.

➤ Government-to-business and government-to-consumer web sites are designed to provide services from the government to the people.

➤ A consumer-to-consumer (C2C) web site enables transactions between consumers. An auction web site is an example of a C2C business model.

➤ A consumer-to-business (C2B) web site is designed to sell products and services to consumers. The distinction of the C2B model from other e-business models is that C2B sites offer permission-based information—the consumer is only presented with information that was requested or pulled off the Internet, not pushed.

➤ An aggregator is a business that act as a middleman for individuals and businesses that want to buy and sell products and services. They help open new markets, increase choices for consumers and business, provide a centralized source for information, and enable comparison-shopping.

➤ A meta-aggregator takes the aggregator service one step further by serving as a broker for the sellers and is able to complete transactions, providing a full-service sales web site.

After completing this lab, you will be able to:

➤ Describe various types of e-businesses

➤ Explain the current types of e-business models being applied today

➤ Identify key factors relating to e-business marketing

13

Materials Required

This lab will require the following:

➤ Windows 98

➤ Internet Explorer 5 or later

➤ Internet access

Estimated completion time: **1 hour**

ACTIVITY

Researching the B2B e-business model:

1. Start **Internet Explorer**.

2. In the Address box, type **http://www.searchebusiness.com**, and then press **Enter**.

3. In the Search text box, type **B2B**, and then press **Enter**.

4. From the search results, find an article that discusses a company that utilizes the B2B e-business model and answer the following questions:

   a. What is the company's name?

   _____

   b. What is the URL?

   _____

   c. Describe the company's product or service.

   _____
   _____
   _____
   _____
   _____

Researching the B2C e-business model:

1. Open **Internet Explorer**.

2. In the Address box, type **http://www.searchebusiness.com**, and then press **Enter**.

3. In the Search text box, type **B2C**, and then press **Enter**.

4. From the search results, find an article that discusses a company that utilizes the B2C e-business model and answer the following questions:

   a. What is the company's name?

   _____

   b. What is the URL?

   _____

   c. Describe the company's product or service.

   _____
   _____
   _____
   _____
   _____

Researching the G2B e-business model:

1. Open **Internet Explorer**.

2. In the Address box, type **http://www.searchebusiness.com**, and then press **Enter**.

3. In the Search text box, type **G2B**, and then press **Enter**.

4. From the search results, find an article that discusses a company that utilizes the G2B e-business model and answer the following questions:

a. What is the company's name?

_____

b. What is the URL?

_____

c. Describe the company's product or service.

_____

_____

_____

_____

_____

Researching the C2C e-business model:

1. Open **Internet Explorer**.

2. In the Address box, type **http://www.searchebusiness.com**, and then press **Enter**.

3. In the Search text box, type **C2C**, and then press **Enter**.

4. From the search results, find an article that discusses a company that utilizes the C2C e-business model and answer the following questions:

a. What is the company's name?

_____

b. What is the URL?

_____

c. Describe the company's product or service.

_____

_____

_____

_____

13

Researching the C2B e-business model:

1. Open **Internet Explorer**.

2. In the Address box, type **http://www.searchebusiness.com**, and then press **Enter**.

3. In the Search text box, type **C2B**, and then press **Enter**.

4. From the search results, find an article that discusses a company that utilizes the C2B e-business and answer the following questions:

a. What is the company's name?

_____

b. What is the URL?

_____

c. Describe the company's product or service.

_____

_____

_____

_____

_____

Researching the B2G e-business model:

1. Open **Internet Explorer**.

2. In the Address box, type **http://www.searchebusiness.com**, and then press **Enter**.

3. In the Search text box, type **B2G**, and then press **Enter**.

4. From the search results, find an article that discusses a company that utilizes the B2G e-business and answer the following questions:

   a. What is the company's name?

   _____

   b. What is the URL?

   _____

   c. Describe the company's product or service.

   _____

   _____

   _____

   _____

   _____

Certification Objectives:

Objectives for the i-Net+ Exam:

➤ Recognize and explain the current types of e-business models being applied today.

➤ Identify key factors relating to strategic marketing considerations as they relate to launching an e-business initiative.

Review Questions

1. A brick-and-click company has both traditional retail stores and an e-business. True or False?

2. One example of an application service provider would be a web-business that sells downloadable music. True or False?

3. B2E web sites do not sell products. True or False?

4. A B2G web site specializes in selling products and services to a government. True or False?

5. An aggregator processes financial transactions between a business and a consumer, whereas a meta-aggregator does not. True or False?

6. *www.ebay.com*, a popular auction web site, is one example of a C2C e-business model. True or False?

LAB 13.2 E-COMMERCE AND TRANSACTION PROCESSING

Objectives

The objective of this lab is to familiarize you with various e-commerce terms and concepts. A web site that can take an order for a product or service can be very simple or very complex. This lab looks at the basic requirements for doing business on the Web and also looks at some of the companies that have emerged to help other companies meet these requirements.

If a transaction involving money happens on a web site, the site uses some form of transaction processing (TP) software, which is software that handles an electronic money transaction. The software can handle all parts of a sale, such as calculating taxes and shipping costs, receiving a credit card number, and posting the transaction to a database. A server on the web site responsible for transaction processing involving money is called an e-commerce server or commerce server. In addition to financial transactions, there are various other types of transactions that occur over the Internet, such as:

13

➤ EFT (Electronic Funds Transfer) is a method of electronically transferring money from one bank to another bank. EFT transactions do not always occur over the Internet.

➤ EBT (Electronic Benefits Transfer) is a method used by government agencies to transfer benefits from a federal account to a retailer.

➤ EDI (Electronic Data Interchange) is a standard format that two computers can use to transfer information when conducting business transactions between institutions, corporations, and governments.

➤ IOTP (Internet Open Trading Protocol) sometimes called OTP, standardizes payment processing for electronic transactions that involve customers, sellers, credit checkers, banks, delivery systems, and other entities.

➤ SET (Secure Electronic Transactions) is a system used to ensure the security of financial transactions on the Internet. When using SET, a user is given a digital certificate. A transaction is processed using a combination of digital signatures and digital certificates to authenticate users and validate the transaction.

After completing this lab, you will be able to:

➤ Define terms related to transaction processing

➤ Be able to describe various types of electronic transactions

➤ Comparison shop and describe how secure online credit card transactions can occur using a third party vendor and a shopping cart program

Materials Required

This lab will require the following:

➤ Windows 98

➤ Internet Explorer 5 or later

➤ Internet access

Estimated completion time: **45 minutes**

ACTIVITY

Research transaction processing:

1. Open **Internet Explorer**.

2. In the Address box, type **http://www.searchebusiness.com**, and then press **Enter**.

3. In the Search text box, type **SET**, and then press **Enter**.

4. Using the information from your search results and your own imagination, describe a scenario in which a company would be implementing SET. Be sure to explain why and how the company would benefit.

_____

_____

_____

_____

_____

_____

_____

_____

_____

_____

Research third-party credit card solutions:

Use the Internet to research three different third-party credit card solutions. You can retrieve information by typing "credit card transactions" into any search engine. Then answer the following questions.

About company #1:

1. What is the company's name?

_____

2. Which credit cards will they allow you to accept on your site?

_____

3. Will they allow you to accept debit cards and checks?

_____

4. What is the price structure?

_____

_____

_____

_____

_____

5. Describe how the company's service could be integrated into a web site. What services and web pages will the vendor provide? What will you have to provide?

_____

_____

_____

_____

_____

_____

_____

_____

_____

13

About company #2:

1. What is the company's name?

_____

2. Which credit cards will they allow you to accept on your site?

_____

_____

3. Will they allow you to accept debit cards and checks?

_____

4. What is the price structure?

_____

_____

_____

_____

_____

5. Describe how the company's service could be integrated into a web site. What services and web pages will the vendor provide? What will you have to provide?

_____
_____
_____
_____
_____
_____
_____
_____
_____

About company #3:

1. What is the company's name?

_____

2. Which credit cards will they allow you to accept on your site?

_____
_____

3. Will they allow you to accept debit cards and checks?

_____

4. What is the price structure?

_____
_____
_____
_____
_____

5. Describe how the company's service could be integrated into a web site. What services and web pages will the vendor provide? What will you have to provide?

_____
_____
_____
_____
_____
_____
_____
_____

Certification Objectives:

Objectives for the i-Net+ Exam:

➤ Understand and be able to describe e-commerce terms and concepts.

Review Questions

1. EDI is a method used to transfer funds between banks. True or False?

2. SET is a system used to ensure the security of financial transactions over the Internet. True or False?

3. EBT is a benefit transfer standard used to transfer employee benefits between employers. True or False?

4. Shopping cart software is required to sell a product or service over the Internet. True or False?

5. From your research, which third-party credit card vendor would you choose and why?

_____

_____

_____

_____

_____

6. From your research, describe how most third-party solutions are linked to a retailer's web site.

_____

_____

_____

_____

13

LAB 13.3 COPYRIGHTS AND TRADEMARKS

Objectives

The legal world is still trying to catch up with the fast growth of the Internet. E-businesses have many of the same problems as traditional businesses regarding protecting their own intellectual properly and respecting the intellectual property of other entities. Unfortunately, with the ease of communication over the Internet, breaking these laws has become easier and more common than ever.

Before beginning this lab, you will need to know the following legal terms:

➤ Jurisdiction has to do with what governmental or other legal body controls the activities of individuals and businesses in a particular region.

➤ A contract, in its simplest form, is an agreement between two parties. A contract is offered by one party and agreed to by another party.

➤ Intellectual property includes ideas and their virtual or physical representations owned by a person, a group of people, a company, or any other legal entity.

➤ A trademark is a name, symbol, or other mark that is used to represent product or a company.

➤ Cybersquatting occurs when someone registers a domain name using another company's trademark or name and then tries to sell the domain name to that company. Cybersquatting was outlawed in 1999.

➤ A copyright is a type of protection that is offered to creators of intellectual property.

➤ A license is a legal tool most often used to sell software. When you purchase software at a retail store, you are actually purchasing a software license to use that software. If you were to actually purchase the software from the company, you would be buying the copyright.

Materials Required

This lab will require the following:

➤ Windows 98

➤ Internet Explorer 5 or later

➤ Internet access

Estimated completion time: **30 minutes**

ACTIVITY
Trademark research:

1. Open **Internet Explorer**.

2. In the Address bar, type **http://www.uspto.gov/**, and then press **Enter**.

3. From the information at this site, describe the difference between a registered and unregistered trademark. Are there any legal disadvantages for not registering a trademark?

_____

_____

_____

_____

_____

_____

_____